All Men Are Not Alike

all men are not alike

Joan Sutton

McClelland and Stewart

Copyright © 1979 by McClelland and Stewart Limited
All rights reserved

The Canadian Publishers
McClelland and Stewart Limited
25 Hollinger Road, Toronto

Printed and bound in the United States of America

CANADIAN CATALOGUING IN PUBLICATION DATA

Sutton, Joan, 1932-
   All men are not alike

Bibliography: p.
ISBN 0-7710-8365-3

1. Men. 2. Interpersonal relations. 3. Love.
I. Title.

HM132.S87   301.41'1   C79-094664-5

For Henry: Like no others

Contents

CHAPTER ONE	My Mother and I	*9*
CHAPTER TWO	Men As Fathers	*18*
CHAPTER THREE	Men As Working Partners	*25*
CHAPTER FOUR	The New Women	*36*
CHAPTER FIVE	Men As Friends	*42*
CHAPTER SIX	Men As Seducers	*52*
CHAPTER SEVEN	Men As Lovers	*60*
CHAPTER EIGHT	Men As Husbands	*72*
CHAPTER NINE	Compulsive Male Personalities	*81*
CHAPTER TEN	Variations in the Male Orgasm	*98*
CHAPTER ELEVEN	What Makes a Good Lover?	*105*
CHAPTER TWELVE	The Loving Men	*113*
	Bibliography	*117*
	Acknowledgements	*119*

CHAPTER ONE

My Mother and I

"The more intelligent a man is, the greater the differences he finds among men. To ordinary persons all men are the same."

Blaise Pascal

My mother used to tell me, "Men are all alike."
 She was as positive about that as she was about the need for me to brush my teeth.
 She was wrong.
 That's just one of the many things that she used to preach that I wish we could rehash, now that I've grown a little older, acquired a perspective of my own and, possibly, enough nerve to talk back. If we could have one of those conversations that are said to sometimes take place between the quick and the dead, I'd challenge her right to make that statement, as well as the statement itself. My mother was, after all, by her own admission a one-man woman.
 Depending on your point of view, you might envy her or pity her for that. Some of you will think her fidelity admirable; others will consider her a fool. The cynics among you will conclude that such fidelity could only be

the result of lack of opportunity, but that was not the case. Even though my mother was trapped by the morality and the restrictions of her time, she was attractive to men and resourceful enough to create both time and opportunity for an affair, had she wished to do so. She was auburn-haired, delicately boned, pretty, with finely shaped hands and tiny feet that were cause for vanity. Vivacious and full of joy, she was a woman of independent spirit who moved to her own music. Its beat was contagious: everyone around her responded to it.

If she was, as she said she was, faithful to her husband, it was surely by choice. One wonders then about that husband, what special magic he had for her, whether there are any men like him left in this world-men powerful enough to bind one woman happily to them for life-and where they might be found.

Her loyalty could imply nights spent in an earthly paradise so erotic that she never wanted to stray, or it could merely have been her way of guaranteeing access to a Presbyterian heaven. But, regardless of its motivation, fidelity does not make a woman an expert on men-one man, maybe, but not men.

Since my mother was not without curiosity or spirit of adventure, she must have wondered what another man would be like. It may be that when she said, "Men are all alike," she was not talking to me at all, but to herself, trying to convince herself that although her world was narrow, she had missed nothing.

It's possible too that she was one of those many women who find themselves attracted over and over again to the same kind of man. That type of repetitive experience reflects a peculiar set of inner compulsions, but in no way can such compulsive behaviour on the part of a woman be said to mirror the nature of men.

She may have sensed the changes in morality that were to shake the post-war world and, instinctively wise, recognized the dangers there would be in sexual liberation for women, especially for her daughter. Perhaps she thought that if she could convince me that all men were the same she would discourage me from experimenting, from wasting my energy and endangering my sense of worth in a frantic search for what we thought of then as the attainable, perfect, dream man.

Whatever. What she told me was wrong. All men are not alike.

I speak with more authority than my mother. Unlike her, I am what is known as a New Woman - a member of a tribe whom society has liberated, first from the role of homemaker, and then from its opposite on the pendulum, Superwoman, that extraordinary creature who was expected to manage everything - husband, career, home, children, the marriage bed - perfectly, without effort or help.

I have been liberated: from the need to bear children or tend to them myself if I do, from baking cakes from scratch, getting married, putting a man's needs, ideas, and opinions first, catering to his wishes, assuming the full responsibility for running his house. As for fidelity - in this liberated world, no one expects a woman to restrict her sexual activities to men, let alone one man. (Or so the literature of liberation would have us believe.)

But my sisters and I were brought up to believe that we should do and be all those traditional things, so it is understandable if, sometimes, we resemble sexual schizophrenics more than we do New Women. We went to the altar in the fifties, wearing virginal white and pledging fidelity. Then came the revolutions - the new morality, the women's movement, marriage breakdown.

Almost overnight the ground rules changed and women were caught in a battlefield of their own making, where upbringing, attitudes, wants, needs and circumstances were all at war. Forgive us if, in the aftermath, we sometimes wonder about the quality of our "liberation." We may have been liberated from the belief that we were created to serve a supportive function to men, but we have not been liberated from the need to love and be loved. And there seems to be some doubt as to whether women can have one without the other.

My life, unlike my mother's, has provided me with enough research material - some of it sought, some of it unsought - to form the basis of a study of men. I have worked for men, with men and I have supervised men. I have seen men in various roles - mentor, husband, lover, son, and friend. I have known, in both the Biblical and the broad sense, more than one man.

At forty-two, after nineteen and a half years of marriage, I separated from the husband who had been my teenage steady and began to lead a half-life - married, but not mated. Used to the certainty that the same man would turn up night after night, reasonably ready in my bed, suddenly there was no man in my bed. And there were two teenagers down the hall.

At forty-six, I became a statistic. Mine was the one out of four marriages waiting for the finality of the divorce court. A mature woman, I found myself thrust from the relative safety of the married state into a world that my mother thought was the exclusive domain of Latin teachers and other spinsters who didn't know how to land a man. My label-conscious generation, accustomed to disguising reality with euphemisms, gave my new status group a glamorous-sounding name - singles - but behind the label lay the truth.

This was a world that was often lonely, sometimes desperate, occasionally without point, and very confusing. Just when my daughter was starting to go out with boys, I was learning to date again. Nothing in my life had prepared me for that moment when my kids would walk me to the door, give a strange man the once-over, and caution, "Don't be late."

I was by then a feminist - not a radical one, but a

believer in equal opportunity and whatever was required to bring that about, as well as equal pay for equal work. I had consciously tried to create a path for other women throughout my professional life and I preached my credo often in my newspaper column. I knew that the women's movement had a long way to go, but I believed without question that it had travelled some distance.

What a shock it was to enter the real world and discover that despite mountains of written material, consciousness-raising, International Women's Year, and an incalculable number of activities meant to improve the status of women, in the world of mating and dating, nothing seemed to have changed since the fifties.

Eventually I did meet some men who had either always been liberated or had been open enough to accept change – men who were secure enough not only to accept but to admire my success; men whose masculinity was not threatened if they had to cook a meal or make a bed; men who were mature enough to prefer adult company; men whose virility did not need to be bolstered and advertised by the company of girls young enough to be their daughters. But that first plunge from the intellectual acceptance of liberation as a revolutionary fact to the reality of a world that still saw initiative as the prerogative of the man was a shock.

I discovered that in most dating situations, the onus was on me to be attractive. At forty-six he was desirable; I was not, unless by some miracle I could manage to look thirty-five. He could, and usually did, have a potbelly, but he was the prize and I was just one very late in entry in the competition: old stretch marks were not allowed. He could be tired from his heavy workload, but no matter how hard I had worked that day or how responsible my role might be on the morrow, on a date I was expected to be the gay and frivolous butterfly. He could be preoccupied by a problem: not me; at six o'clock I was to be scintillating, and ready to divert with soothing conversation or to provide a listening, adoring – certainly never critical - ear. He could come from the office without changing his shirt or having a shower, but my part in the play dictated that I be perfumed and prettied, like a ham going to the table. If he wanted something from me, either sex or companionship or a soothing interlude, he could call on me at the last moment. But I was not expected to initiate a date or to articulate any needs. If I did, I was demanding. It was all right, however, for me to take the initiative by leading him on with a coy flirtatious game or a pretence of helplessness.

Women's lib: what was that?

At the other extreme, there were men who found in liberation the realization of a fantasy. There was no longer any need for them to demonstrate courtly manners, no need for them to pick up the dinner cheque. But it was expected that after dinner, I would be dessert.

I found myself wondering who had been liberated, from what, and for what? It seemed to me that most of the advantages of liberation had gone to men.

At forty-six, my date was expected to have *achieved*, for professional success added to his appeal. Certainly if he was divorced, no one blamed that on his business accomplishments. It was assumed instead that his wife had failed to keep up with him in personal or social growth. But my success was suspect. There were many men (and some women) who concluded that I had put my work ahead of my marriage, that I was ambitious (an unattractive adjective when applied to a woman), a workoholic, a driven female whose essential femininity was in question because I did not have a man whom society could call my own.

Consciousness-raising had been going on to the point of boredom, it seemed. But little of it had penetrated the thinking of many of the men of my generation. At sixteen, I had lost a beau when I defeated him in a debate. Thirty years later, many of the men I met were still threatened by ability in a woman. These men were unable to deal with the attention my status as a minor celebrity attracted from headwaiters. They were made insecure by financial independence. Traditionalists, they were accustomed to women who were dependent on them financially, emotionally, socially.

That kind of dependence on the part of their women enhanced these men's images of themselves as men. They could not imagine that there might be a better, more rewarding, richer basis for a relationship. Those who could were suspicious of the possibilities. Instinctively, perhaps, they recognized that a relationship between equals had its own demands. For many men, those commitments - true intimacy and the gift of self - would be harder to meet than those inherent in the traditional protector-dependent version of the male-female relationship.

My dating experiences exposed me to the various attitudes of individual men, but my first detached exposure to large groups of men came in response to my work as a columnist for a Toronto newspaper. Although it was generally assumed that mine was a women's column, hundreds of men wrote letters to me. Some were from men angry at me because they detected an assumption on my part that women had a monopoly on feeling; some were from men who had been hurt; others were from men who were psychologically threatened by my exposure of my emotions. Some came from men who thought - usually erroneously but very revealingly - that I was writing about them. And some came from media groupies who wanted to take me out, to be seen with me. Some writers were caricatures of the male myth, macho to the extreme. Others were sentimental romantics, lost in a world where men were denied the right to exhibit tenderness.

Read in total, those letters reveal how individualistic

men are: their needs, their wants, their responses, their expectations, and their follies are, like Cleopatra's, infinite in their variety. Read in total, they brought to the fore some attitudes that had been buried in my subconscious. I realized that while I had denied intellectually my mother's dictum about men being alike, on one level I had believed her. As many women had, I too assumed that men were the same sexually. I had bought the old cliché that a man was always ready for sex; that a man could easily separate the emotional and the physical; and I certainly believed that an erection meant desire, and that ejaculation meant satisfaction.

The letters made me curious. Later, interviews with doctors, therapists, and sexologists helped me to understand the physiology and the psychology of men. How removed the truth is from the myth!

While this was happening in my professional life, my son was growing up and, watching him, I learned even more about men. He had one face for the world – the face demanded of him by his peers – but behind it I caught glimpses of touching vulnerability. He had the sexual initiative that women coveted; he paid for it in painful exposure to rejection. The macho bravado that he occasionally donned was a shell that made him a member of his tribe, but it was never quite thick enough to protect him from his own very human sensitivities.

His willingness to embrace automatically certain male attitudes is not unusual, nor is such need for peer approval restricted to adolescence. Many men deliberately hide their differences in a collective, stereotyped response that does not reflect their true beliefs, but does guarantee them membership – and acceptance – in the male club. Stag parties are a good example of such behaviour. Despite the repugnance that some men clearly have for the vulgarity of such events, few of them would ever admit to that in the presence of other men.

Most men are also compelled by their own insecurity to

try to perpetuate the traditional balance of power between the sexes. The methods they use to achieve that in their personal lives are, however, various indeed. In this book, I examine some of those techniques, as well as the ways in which men vary at home, at work, and in bed. For once you get past the power games and the rituals perpetuated for peer acceptance, you soon discover that men may be alike in their membership in the human race, but they are different in every other way. Good, bad, amoral, boring, fascinating, wicked, saintly, responsible, immature, kind, malicious, faithful, promiscuous, stingy, generous, tender, violent, hetero, homo, sexless, sexy: name it and the quality is found in both genders.

That may seem like a simplistic discovery, but the myths of the sexes are deeply ingrained. Even when men and women recognize intellectually that each sex dips into the common well of humanity, emotionally we still tend to think of the members of the opposite sex in generalities – particularly when we are having a problem with one of them.

CHAPTER 2

Men As Fathers

"The father-daughter relationship provided an added dimension to these women's childhoods. From it they drew attention, approval, reward and confirmation. It was an added source of early learning, a very early means of expanding their experience, and through it they gained a role model with which they could begin to identify.

Margaret Hennig and Anne Jardim,
The Managerial Woman

A father's role varies throughout nature as well as history. In the world of fish, the stickleback is an exemplary father. He not only helps to prepare the nest, but protects and oxygenates the eggs and then guards the young after hatching. Most male birds will help to build a nest in territory that they have won and are prepared to defend, and they will share in the incubation and feeding of the young. Certain caged rhesus monkeys take fatherhood beyond caretaking; they are willing to cuddle and play with their progeny.

But basically, fatherhood that goes beyond the planting of sperm is primarily a characteristic of human beings. The role of father in the human family varies, from culture to culture and from one period in history to another. Our Western image of the father's role is largely influenced by our Judeo-Christian heritage. Within that tradition there are many versions of how that role should be played. There are some who embrace the patriarchal view of father as the last, supreme authority, a man detached from emotion. Our Puritan background, which suggests that the role of a father is to go out and make a good living for his family and leave domestic issues to the women in the household, endorses that view. But, with the male role in so many areas being reappraised, fatherhood too is receiving some scrutiny. There are many men and women today who believe that a father should take an active role in parenting, from being in the delivery room to assisting in every aspect of child care.

FATHERS AS DISPOSABLE PARENTS
Much of society's attitude to parenting in the first part of this century is the result of the work of Freud. He charged women with the responsibility for the emotional nutrition and loving care of children, while men were given the task of paying the bills and administering discipline. Behind this Freudian philosophy there are some assumptions about women: an assumption that inside every woman there is a maternal instinct waiting to be unleashed automatically with the birth of a child; that women are made to be mothers, always willing to put their own needs, ambitions, and desires second to those of their children.

Men, on the other hand, are assumed to be detached from parenting. They plant the sperm, but no one expects a man to feel the pull of the umbilical cord. These attitudes have produced a society in which fathers are all too often treated like disposable parents. Women claim the right to abortions – without any consideration of the feelings or desires of the man who participated in the creation of the child. The courts, lagging behind attitudinal changes, still tend to give custody of children to the mother, whether or not she is in fact the best person to raise the child. When custody is denied to her it is usually because she had been branded an unfit mother, seldom simply because the father would be the better parent.

When a separation or a divorce takes place, fathers are usually relegated to a secondary role and given minimal visitation rights at specific times. In some cases, they are denied access to their children.

Now we are beginning to realize how unfair these arbitrary assumptions are to everybody, especially to the children. Every child needs two parents; every child wants to know, love, and be loved by two parents. Fathers are important - just as important as mothers.

Studies indicate that mothers and fathers each bring unique gifts to parenthood. In infancy, it is the father who encourages a child to explore and to solve problems, while the mother's protective instinct tends to inhibit such activities. In adolescence, it is the child's relationship to the father - sexual rivalry in the case of a boy, sexual interest in the case of a girl - that encourages the cord-cutting that is essential to becoming an adult.

FATHERS AND DAUGHTERS

A father's active role, or his absence, helps to shape a girl's personality. Her relationship with her father largely determines how comfortably she accepts herself as a female. In order to have a loving relationship with a man of her own age, it is important that there first be a comfortable, loving relationship with her father. Deprived of that, she may idealize her father and seek out someone similar to him to love. In some cases, she goes through life unable to be satisfied, never able to make up for the love and approval that was absent when she was growing up.

While a mother often tends to treat both sons and daughters in the same way, fathers are likely to differentiate. Consequently it is in her relationship with her father that a girl first defines acceptable feminine behaviour, as well as her future pattern of behaviour with men. There is evidence to suggest that lesbians had fathers who were hostile, puritanical, exploitive, possessive, and infantilizing.

There is even evidence to suggest that a woman's relationship to her father may influence her success in her professional life. In *The Managerial Woman*, a study of twenty-five women who became company presidents, Margaret Hennig and Anne Jardim wrote, "All had had extremely close relationships with their fathers and had been involved in an unusually wide range of traditionally masculine activities in the company of their fathers, beginning when they were very young."

SINGLE-PARENT FATHERS
There are some men, just as there are some women, who seem to be able to walk away from their children and forget them. But most men, even though they may not know how to show it or articulate it, feel the pull of parenthood very strongly. When they are denied the right to participate in parenting, they experience grief and pain. Some even attempt to kidnap their children.

Roles are changing, and the myth of motherhood is being challenged. We are seeing that there are some women who do not want to be mothers; some who discover that they don't like, let alone love, their babies; some who find that they cannot handle the day-in, day-out pressure of child care. More of them are finding the courage to admit to these feelings, even though society still views such women as unnatural monsters. Sometimes, these women bring their husbands actively into the act of parenting, sharing with them all aspects of child care, from the delivery room to school parents' nights, bed-time baths, and stories. Others run away, leaving their children in the custody of fathers. Seven per cent of single-parent families are now headed by men.

These men face and cope with the same problems as single-parent mothers do – how to find day care, how to manage work and a home, how to satisfy sexual needs without confusing the children. Yet society still refuses to recognize that men can be good caretakers of children. Although financial support is available to women who choose to stay home to be full-time mothers, in Ontario there is no similar assistance available to men who choose to stay home to be full-time fathers.

Single-parent fathers tend to remarry quickly. Instead of solving their problems, this tactic often adds to them. The new wife may not be able to be loving to children who are strangers; mixing two families together may result in a conflict over discipline, or guilt about sharing time and money with someone else's children.

Society's traditional attitude to fathers has resulted in men who have been emotionally shortchanged and deprived of some of the best aspects of parenting-the loving, the caring, the emotional feedback. In some cases, the wives deliberately foster this disparity. After all, if a woman's power base is her hold on her children, it is not surprising that, in some cases, she exploits it. Many a wife of a straying husband recognizes that the children are the ace in her particular suit of cards. She makes it clear that if hubby leaves, he risks losing the affection of his children, because she controls that; their perception of their father has always been filtered through her interpretation of him.

Sometimes the mother's actions are unconscious, even well-intentioned: "Don't bother daddy, he's busy," or "Leave daddy alone, he's tired." Many women isolate their husbands from their children by conspiring against them: "Yes, I'll do that, but let's not tell daddy, he wouldn't understand." Others cast him as the big stick: "Wait till your father gets home and I tell him what you did."

DIVORCED FATHERS

That background produces a father who has no real relationship with his children, a father who has never talked about anything that matters with his kids, a father who doesn't know his children, and children who do not know their father. If a separation takes place in this kind of family, the father is at a loss. He has always depended on his wife to organize the personal side of family life. How does he begin? He has no base on which to build a continuing relationship with his children.

This dad assumes that it is not enough for his kids to be with him; they must do something with him. His time with his family becomes scheduled and busy, revolving around trips and outings. There is no room for spontaneity, for quiet talk, for just enjoying each other. He may feel that he has to be Santa Claus, buying the affection of his children with expensive gifts.

The adversary system that prevails in most divorce actions does not take into consideration the real needs of children. The spouses forget that they may be able to divorce each other, but they cannot divorce themselves from their children - or should not. Wise couples will recognize that each parent has a continuing role to play in the child's life and they will do their best to facilitate that continuity in as natural a manner as possible.

Today the obstacles to fatherhood in single-parent families are so severe that many fathers become discouraged and allow relationships with their children to die out. Contrived, scheduled visitations tend to become a chore for both parent and child. Sometimes, the father deludes himself into believing that letting go is the best solution for everybody. In fact, the best solution is an environment in which the child is given permission to continue a relationship with each of his parents. Even if the custodial parent remarries, there should be no attempt to shut the natural parent out and regroup around the step-parent. Studies indicate that children who have healthy relationships with their natural parents develop healthy relationships with their step-parents much more easily.

Obviously, divorce is painful for everyone. Unfortunately, the two adults who are going through it often become so absorbed in their own pain, guilt, and recriminations that they forget that the children, too, are suffering from the shock that follows in the wake of divorce. At the time when kids need their parents most, the adults are often too emotionally exhausted to be able to provide parenting.

Whether the marriage is intact or over, mothers should not shut fathers out, no matter how great the temptation. And when fathers are shut out, either by the mother or the child, they should be persistent, determined to claim both the rights and the responsibilities of parenthood.
It's time that society recognized the capacity of men to love their children, to care for them in other than material and disciplinary ways, to influence their self-image. Of all the myths that surround the male mystique, the myth that says fatherhood ends with conception - that men can't be caring parents, that fathers are not fit to take the responsibility for raising their children - is one of the most destructive.

CHAPTER 3

Men As Working Partners

"We know that having ability to achieve in management careers is not the result of being born a man, but how does a man whose career success has confirmed for him his masculine identity now give up this confirmation? Can he even be expected to try?"

Margaret Hennig and Anne Jardim,
The Managerial Woman

Working with men, for men or, in some cases, supervising men, presents special problems for a woman. There are some women who put all their energy into raving over the fact that gender-oriented problems shouldn't exist in the business world. It is my opinion that the woman who wants to succeed in business should accept those problems as the reality of life in the workforce and, instead of fighting them, she should learn to deal with them effectively.

Men made the rules for the business world; women are the newcomers. When a woman aims for a place in middle or upper management, she must learn to work within the rules already established or she will fail. Women are gaining acceptance in the corporate structure, but it is a reluctant acceptance. So long as men are not sure that they want us in their bailiwick, they are not about to change the rules in order to make it easier for us to succeed. The woman who chooses to try to change the rules along the way may become a feminist heroine, and she may bring about some small token future improvement for other women; but she will be labelled a strident troublemaker and find herself cut off by men from advancement and the rewards of business – as well as from the opportunity to share those rewards with other women.

At work, men and women have different attitudes, different values and, in some cases, different goals. Whether those differences are the result of genes or conditioning is for the experts to decide and the behavioural scientists to change. Why there are differences is irrelevant to the woman who is in competition with men today. Whether the situation is fair or unfair is equally irrelevant. All that matters is the reality. A woman who makes it into the ranks of top management must be clear-eyed and clear-headed about that reality. Once she gets to the top, she can change the rules. But on the way up, she has to play the game as it exists.

THE REALITY

Unfair expectations are part of the reality of the game. More is expected of a woman professionally, at every level. Just to bring herself to the attention of management she will have to demonstrate greater ability than her male peers. Men are accustomed to thinking of other men as material for promotion but, even though more and more companies are aggressively creating places for women, it may still be necessary for an ambitious woman to pinpoint, articulate, and pursue her management goal, constantly reminding her superiors of her presence and her ability. All the way up the ladder, she will be permitted fewer mistakes, and the mistakes she does make will be weighed, not just against her, but against the women who would follow in her path.

Male discomfort is another reality: there are many

men who, for various reasons, are uncomfortable about the idea of making a place for women at the top. The executive who is sincere about his interest in promoting female talent may be uncomfortable about his investment in the training of such a woman. Is she serious about her career? Committed to it for her whole working life? How will marriage and family affect her ambitions? How easily can she be transferred? Those are not male-female questions; they are human questions. But men do not ask them of men; they do ask them of women. It is up to women to confront those issues and provide the reassurance that is needed.

There are some men who are uncomfortable about the possible effect a woman may have on their behaviour. Will they still be able to swear, tell off-colour stories, comment on the receptionist's boobs, and smoke cigars? Usually, men find that this anxiety has no basis in reality. Although they have reserved for themselves the right to behave like jocks, in actual fact, at a business meeting they seldom do. Their locker-room vulgarity exists (as do so many other locker-room attributes) only in their heads.

Where jock behaviour does exist, it is important for a woman to remember that playing the game by men's rules does not mean that she should become one of the boys. That's not in the game plan. The woman with career-smarts does not tell the dirtiest joke or use the most swear words; neither does she faint or express shock or indignation. The best reaction is no reaction: she is too busy with her thoughts to hear. Eventually, her presence will be accepted and, if she has made a contribution, it will be valued. Then, if there is a need, one man will likely take it upon himself to improve the standard of behaviour in the others.

If she is the first woman to join a particular group, there may be a tendency to give her an exaggerated impression of vulgar male behaviour as a kind of initiation rite, an expression of the "if-you-can't-stand-the-heat-get-out-of-the-kitchen" school of thought. In that respect, this can be a tough time for women. The women's movement is in transition: women have lost the traditional forms of respect that men once automatically paid them and they have not yet won respect of another kind. They are not yet regarded as equal contributors.

A man will be uncomfortable with a woman if she is after his job or in competition with him for the same promotion. There is not much she can do to alleviate that discomfort except to make it clear that she will compete on ability, not on sex appeal. The very idea that women are competing, let alone that they might win, threatens men with a menace that extends beyond the workplace. When a man loses to a woman, he loses something more than a job; he loses his image of himself as the superior, dominant, protective sex. In the era of the vibrator and sperm banks, men are entitled to wonder whether there is a place for them in a liberated world; entitled to worry about giving up their established role before they know what their new role will be.

SEXUAL HARASSMENT

Every career woman is subject to some form of sexual harassment. In its most blatant form, it is practised by a supervisor who insists that a woman "put out" in order to keep her job or get a raise.

That kind of sexual harassment is not a game played only by men. There are women who deliberately use their sex appeal or who become intimate with a senior executive in the hope that the relationship will provide a short-cut to the top.

But sexual harassment is not always as blatant as a supervisor's demand that a woman become intimate with him. More often, it is expressed in an infuriating barrage of personal, sex-oriented remarks, or pats on the bottom, or a hand that somehow always brushes the breast. There may be a patronizing assumption that a female can't read the bottom line, understand a profit-and-loss statement, drive a van, or sit in a meeting without wanting to make the coffee. Sometimes the harassment is even more subtle - and much harder to deal with. When a woman is impatient or demanding, there will be some who will suggest that she is having her period, in the menopause, starved for sex, or neurotic because she's having man trouble.

There are, of course, some men and women working partners who become involved with each other not out of intimidation or threats but because they are attracted to each other. When that kind of relationship ends, it is the woman who inevitably must change jobs, either because she cannot bear being near someone with whom she might be in love; because her presence embarrasses her former lover; or because the man's wife has insisted on the mistress's departure as part of the terms of reconciliation. Management usually comes down on the side of the man, sometimes because of male bonding, often because, even when a woman must work for financial reasons, her need is not taken as seriously.

THE IMAGE GAME
When a woman works with men who see her first as female and then as talent, she cannot win in the image game. Men know that their minds can be compartmentalized and that they can separate their private and professional lives. But it doesn't occur to them that a woman can do that, too. If she is detached, professional, and excels, she will be labelled unfeminine, a bitch, and a ball-breaker. ("Who would want to live with that?") If she retains her femininity, she will be thought of as emotional, manipulative, not hard-nosed enough for top management. The best example of this syndrome is Margaret Thatcher, the recently elected Prime Minister of Great Britain. Despite the fact that Mrs. Thatcher is married

and the mother of two children, the predominantly male press dubbed her The Iron Maiden, suggesting that any woman as strong-minded as Mrs. Thatcher must be sexless, inflexible, and without feeling. But when she admitted to an interviewer that at the end of a particularly tough day she sometimes cried, there were editorials written by the same group of men suggesting that her tears made her unfit to be Prime Minister. Neither view hindered Mrs. Thatcher's success. She was too busy succeeding to bother commenting on the unfairness of such pendulum-swings in judgement.

Men themselves cannot measure up to the strict standards by which they measure women, for even men give in to their humanity once in a while. Men are often more protective of an unproductive employee or an old loyalty (of the male variety, anyway) than women are. Certainly men are not above the use of emotion as a tool to get their way. I have worked for men who took everything – from a disagreement over policy to a decision to quit – personally; men who questioned my loyalty when I questioned their judgement; and one who, when he disagreed with me, pointedly called me by his wife's name.

Since there are still very few women in top management in any field, if a woman wants to join that circle she needs the support and assistance of men. To get that, she must be well trained, with impeccable credentials, more than competent in her job, and professional in her dress and manner. And she has to avoid both office politics and office romances.

She will also learn to handle men, even though she will sometimes resent the energy that that takes. She will think twice before shooting down a male coworker's idea in an open meeting. A man can do that to another man and be applauded for his clear thinking, his contribution to the company, and his courage in speaking out; but when a woman attacks a man's idea, she is seen to be attacking not the idea but the man.

Sometimes there is an automatic, initial collective male resistance to anything new put forward by a woman. If she is trying to promote some plan, project, or policy that is essential for her success, she will enlist some male support in advance to make sure that the idea is approved. Sometimes she will persuade a man who will be in attendance to present it for her. That strategy has to be weighed carefully. If the idea is the important thing and credit for it counts, then she must find some way to present it herself and to convert the group to her cause. But if the idea is important only in that it will permit her to do something even more significant, then she can afford to let someone else have the credit. The long-range benefits will still be hers.

She must learn to play the team game, a concept that is foreign to many women unless they attended girls' private schools, where there is an emphasis on intramural sports. Females often tend to concern themselves with individuals: whether they like or dislike a certain person, what that person's values are. These issues might matter to a man privately, but in business he's prepared to work with anyone who can help land an account, please a client, increase the shareholder's profits, or help him get ahead – whether he likes that person or not.

Compromise – a day-to-day reality in business – is to many women a dirty word. Recently, the senior executive of a major corporation was able to convince his board to include women in a new management-training program. A female business graduate with outstanding qualifications was selected. At the end of a month she quit, complaining that she didn't respect her supervisor. The effect of that fiasco will be felt by other women in that company for some time. All the fine courses in economics and administration were wasted on that young woman. No one taught her the rules of the game. When you have learned all you can learn in a job, gone as far as you can go, you should go on to something better, even if you like the company and your boss. But until then, you do not openly challenge the qualifications of a superior. Even if senior management thinks that the junior employee is right, they will side with one of their own.

The Old Boys' Network works against some men and all women – not deliberately, but effectively. Men do help each other. The old school or club tie does carry with it a strong bond of loyalty and, even though men may not actually do business on the golfcourse, they do use that locale to cement a friendship, plant an idea, and put in a plug for a friend. Few women are ever admitted to a golfing foursome, but they can hone their competitive talents and win some respect from male peers on the tennis courts. Men admire tough competitors.

There's an even more select and lucrative level to which women are denied access. If a woman wants to gain admission to that very private group where she might be given stock options, the opportunity to take an equity position in a new company, or be named to a Board of Directors, she must build solidly, step by step, earning trust and respect, as well as a reputation for moderate, sensible, discreet behaviour.

Enlightened managers are making room for women; they are looking for women to fill top positions; and they are giving those women the opportunity to learn. A male executive in this kind of company does not fault a woman for her inexperience, because he realizes that for years women have been denied the opportunity to acquire experience. He may be the rare man who has always seen women as people of worth. He may be a man whose consciousness has been raised by parenthood; if he is a father of daughters, he will probably not want doors to be closed to them. He will not stake his affirmative-action program for women on the basis of the performance of a token woman, nor will he judge all women who come after her by her failures.

He is also a rare breed. Most women's male bosses fall in one of five categories.

THE MEN WOMEN WORK FOR

Big Daddy: He sees himself as Santa Claus. Every raise, fringe benefit, and day off is a personal present from him, a treat given, not by the company, but at his whim. In return, he demands unquestioning personal loyalty. He will expect you to get involved in company politics on his side and he may expect you to perform daughterly duties, like picking up his laundry, reminding him of his wife's birthday, or organizing the menu for a luncheon meeting. Never mind that you are not his secretary or his mistress. You are a woman, dependent on him, and he has been generous with you. Be grateful.

The Blinkered Horse: He's willing to concede that, despite the fact that you are a woman, you have ability. But you are the exception. In no way will he rethink his opinion of women as a group in the workforce. He will tell you with great enthusiasm that you think like a man. Don't ask him, "Which man?" He won't understand.

Critical-Path-Method Mike: Business-wise, this man is with-it! He speaks the lingo of the trade, to the bewilderment of all who hear. He cannot understand anything unless it is presented in graph or chart form. And he is wild about reports – especially twenty-page tomes that are circulated internally for the express purpose of reminding everyone how busy and important he is. He is always in a meeting. Resist your feminine impulse to simplify things. This man measures his importance by his paper output and the number of meetings on his calendar.

Depression Dan: He doesn't believe that women have to work, and he clings to that belief in the face of statistics that prove otherwise. He'll never say it, but he is convinced that you work for the fun of it, and that instead of taking a salary, you should pay the company. If anyone has to be cut from staff, he believes it should be the woman, regardless of her seniority or her merits. He resents having to pay a woman the same money he pays a man, even if she does the same work equally well or better. The law obliges him to do that, but he never considers her when he is doling out fringe benefits like a company car, an expense account, or a corner office. Resist that other feminine instinct – the one that says status doesn't matter. In the male business world, you are only as important as your status symbols. Get them!

The Mentor: Lucky is the woman who finds one boss like this. He recognizes talent and ability and takes pride in helping to develop it. He may lift such a person out of the ranks and make her a special assistant, sharing with her his thought processes, letting her make more and more decisions, and making it clear to others that she is producing specific contributions. Finally, when she is ready, he pushes her out of the nest to fly through doors he has helped to open, armed with references, contacts, knowledge, and experience.

THE MEN WHO WORK FOR WOMEN
There are still some men who emphatically declare that they will not work for a woman. Not many say so, because articulating something like that is not fashionable today. Whether the sentiment is spoken or not, it exists in violation of the rules of the game that men themselves created. A woman who will work with anyone who can help her achieve her objective is said to be "thinking like a man"; so surely the opposite is true: a man who will not work for a woman, regardless of her qualifications, is not thinking the way a man, in the game he created, should be prepared to do.

Almost all men will work with a woman if her approach is maternal. If she babies him, humours him, coaxes work out of him, and fixes up his problems, he will be content indeed; he has an office mother. If she is an editor, that is a reasonable approach to take, one that she may well take with both male and female employees. But if she's a management trainee, she will usually find that her male employees have skipped over her head and been promoted beyond her, while she is left to wet-nurse the next group of trainees. Company presidents seldom come from the ranks of mother hens.

A man who is genuinely tuned in to the techniques of career success is prepared, however, to work for anybody, male or female, who can deliver challenges, opportunities, and credit. If a female boss is on the way up, she can take her department with her. If she delegates responsibility and gives credit where it is due, her employees will share in her success. And, if she can be promoted and move on to the next job without clinging to her old responsibilities, she will create a management vacancy for someone else-perhaps for the man who works for her. Everyone likes to work for a boss like that.

CHAPTER 4

The New Women

"Women tend to make their emotions perform the functions they exist to serve, and hence remain mentally much healthier than men."

Ashley Montagu, *The Natural Superiority of Women*

Our relationships with our fathers and male professional associates are relatively straightforward, compared to the thorny tangle of male-female interaction on other levels. Regardless of the nature of the relationship, one sex should not form an opinion of the other in isolation. We should not judge men without also considering the nature of women, for how men behave is very much influenced by the behaviour of women. Consequently, to my own experiences as an incipient divorcee, a newspaper columnist, a businesswoman, and the mother of a son, I have added the candid reminiscences of six other women.

Some of these women have had concurrent multiple sexual relationships, some have been faithful to one man at a time on a sequential basis, and one has had sexual relations only with her husband. They have all been exposed to a large number of men, either as friends or lovers, husbands, or would-be seducers.

ANNE

Forty-six, married once, divorced once, Anne is one of the few women I know who candidly admits that she was not a virgin when she married. She lost that symbol of innocence in the back seat of a car, in a coupling so unremarkable that she remembers asking her mate, "Have you finished?"

Before she married that man – and it is perhaps significant that she married the man who claimed her virginity, in however undistinguished a manner – she carried on a passionate sexual affair with another man for two years. She also took part in three one-night stands – one in a motel, two in cars – with men whose names she has forgotten.

During her twenty-two-year marriage, she had three sequential affairs. Each lasted about three years and in each case, she confined her sexual activities to that lover and her husband. Somehow, in between, she found time and opportunity to go to bed at least once – and sometimes more often – with twenty-two other men.

There were mementos: two abortions, a mild bout of venereal disease, and a severe case of *déjà vu*. She could not, even in this age of liberation, be considered typical, but the range of her experience – sexual contact with thirty men – does qualify her to comment on the question, "Are all men alike?" Her answer is no.

BETTINA

Bettina is a jet-setting international beauty, now sixty years of age. She adhered strictly to her generation's definition of morality; she did not sleep with a man before marriage. Bettina has had six husbands – two of whom died, three whom she divorced, and one who divorced her.

Because of her beauty, she has been actively courted. Because she managed to control her emotions and knew how to market her assets, she is now a very wealthy woman with an apartment on Fifth Avenue in New York City, an island in Northern Ontario, a flat in London, England, and a villa in Spain. Ask her if all men are alike and she will reply, with some amusement in her voice, "No!"

CAROLINE

Caroline is forty. She was a seventeen-year-old virgin when she leaped into marriage with the first man who could take her away from the stifling village in northern England where she grew up. When she was nineteen, she realized that if she was to fulfil her ambitions for herself, she would have to leave him, too.

An ocean away, she worked her way up the corporate ladder in a job that offered opportunity for travel. For five years, she commuted between New York, Chicago, Toronto, and Los Angeles. In each city, she found a male companion who would buy her dinner, take her dancing, and bed her. Although these men never paid her for her sexual favours the way they would have paid a prostitute, they always bought her expensive presents. She accepted them without hesitation because she loved beautiful things, couldn't afford to buy them for herself, and felt that her role of sexual Lady Bountiful entitled her to them.

She remarried in 1968, continuing to travel in her job. For two years she maintained her various casual sexual encounters. Then several things happened. Her husband began to make a lot of money and she no longer needed other men to provide the baubles that reassured her that she had indeed travelled a long way from the poverty of her youth. Various news stories heightened her sense of the danger that there might be behind a closed door with a stranger. Amoral for years, she suddenly discovered morality in the form of guilt. She regretted deceiving her husband. For the first time, she felt the stirring of responsibility that is love and decided to be faithful, not for the sake of fidelity, but because she wanted to intensify her marital relationship. For the past eight years, she has been a one-man woman. That, more than anything else, has convinced her that all men are not alike. If they were, her husband would not be unique. And, she says, he is.

DIANE

Diane is twenty-five, unmarried. She almost lost her virginity at seventeen, but couldn't figure out how to insert a diaphragm. Her impatient Romeo tried to help, but the results – then tragic, now comic – killed desire on both their parts. One wonders whether he went on to be a gynecologist; she went on to master the mechanics of birth control and, a year later, the deed was done under more romantic circumstances.

Diane has to be "in love" to have sex. That has happened to her three times. In between, she has been pursued by many men, both young and old. She has covered the singles-bar scene (and rejected it), and she has spent some time without any man in her life. She is now living with her lover and they are considering marriage because she wants to have children. Each man who has approached her has been different – in his techniques, his needs, his responses, and in his ability to make a commitment.

EDNA

Edna is fifty years old and is only now losing her innocence about men. Married at twenty to her first boyfriend, she remained devoted, loving, faithful, and content throughout her marriage. Widowed a year, she still has not had sex with another man. She is, however, being actively pursued – clandestinely – by several of her husband's married friends and some of her friends' husbands. She has two open suitors, a sixty-year-old widower and a divorced man her own age. Becoming single again has forced her to recognize that all men are not alike. Some see her only as an outlet for sex; others are aware of her as a total person.

FRANCES

Frances is a thirty-year-old married secretary who six months before I interviewed her began an affair with her boss – her first infidelity. She is still having sexual relations with her husband, although she finds that repugnant. She believes that eventually she and her lover will leave their respective spouses, divorce, and remarry.

At work, Frances has daily contact with ten men, some of whom see her as a possible sexual conquest, some of whom see her as a slave, and some of whom confide in her as a friend.

Frances joins the chorus of women who adamantly declare, "All men are not alike."

You may, of course, be tempted to turn this evidence around and judge these women on the basis of their sexual activity, but that is not what this book is about.

You may also claim that this book is one-sided, and it is. Any of the men who unwittingly contributed to its research could claim, "But that isn't how it was" – and they might be right. In human relationships, there is no objective truth. Because of that, this book does not pretend to be based on anything resembling scientific truth. It is instead a book about perceptions – how one group of women perceive men and, equally important, how they see men perceiving themselves.

Undoubtedly, the women's perceptions differ from what the men believe is the reality of the situation. But each of us is several people – the person we believe ourselves to be, the person we really are, and the person others perceive us to be. No matter how great the discrepancy, each version is true: if we are to understand ourselves and each other we must come to know each of those images and find a way to integrate them.

The women in this book have been open and honest and, even though I have disguised their identities, such candour puts them at risk. Despite that, they agreed to contribute to the following chapters because they would like to facilitate that integration of images. They feel that much of what goes on between men and women today is dishonest, and they would like to help bring about a more realistic dialogue between the sexes.

CHAPTER 5

Men As Friends

*"What lasting joys the man attend
Who has a polished female friend."*

Anonymous

The rarest and most precious feeling that can grow between a man and a woman is friendship.

If, when my mother said that all men were alike, she was implying that all men wanted only one thing - sex - from a woman, she was very wrong: friendship is a glorious possibility. Sometimes that friendship becomes the springboard for a sexual love, sometimes it is an outgrowth of sexual love, a fringe benefit of a dying or dead affair. But friendship can also grow, even where the relationship is determinedly non-sexual.

Admittedly, non-sexual friendship between a man and a woman is rare, for several reasons - some of them very practical. Many women just don't have the opportunity to meet men and get to know them well enough for friendship to develop. Although more and more women are entering the workforce and thereby expanding the number of their male acquaintances, about half of the adult women in North America still live lives bound by children, school, home, family, female friends. The men they meet are business acquaintances or friends of their husbands, or husbands of their friends. In our society as it exists today, there is little opportunity within this circle to develop male friendships without threatening the woman's own marriage or the marriage of someone else.

Few women – and even fewer men – have developed the skills that co-educational friendship requires. In North America, men and women still see each other first as sexual objects. Many women are compelled to turn every encounter into a flirtation; they read a sexual advance into every greeting. They deliberately hide their serious, thoughtful sides (especially their strengths) in order to meet the stereotype of the feminine, helpless female.

Many men are extremely uncomfortable with a woman outside her traditional role as wife, mother, lover, or potential lover. The idea that a woman could be a friend has never occurred to them. Men who see the male-female pattern as a dominant-submissive one cannot permit an equal exchange of possibly conflicting ideas between themselves and a woman, even in friendly conversation. A man who is compelled to "put a woman in her place" cannot be a friend to her, because to his mind she is an inferior. The man who perceives all women to be alike will not recognize the face of friendship when it is attached to a female body. The man who thinks of every woman as a sexual challenge can never see her as a person. These men feel many emotions about women – love, lust, a desire to protect, subdue, or conquer. But they have never learned to *like* a woman.

The men who do like women are splendid human beings, men of many dimensions. One of my favourite male friends would easily meet the standards that other men apply when they are measuring one of their own. Paul is a success in the male-dominated corporate world.

He came to retirement with a brilliant business record, then went on to become chairman of another company, leading it through difficult times. He is a sportsman, an adventurer, a sailor, an excellent tennis player, and he is definitely heterosexual. He and his first wife raised a large family in a happy environment. Several years after her death, he married a younger, glamorous, unorthodox woman of strong opinions. They have a large circle of friends and live a life rich in varied interests.

Paul likes women. He is an expert at flirting but his interest in women goes beyond that. He appreciates the way they think, and at a party he seeks women out to talk about all the many things that interest him – politics, literature, the theatre, history, sociology, film, the world. He will talk business in general, with men or women, but he has a rule that he does not talk about the specifics of his own business with anyone after five o'clock. He is what I call a modern Renaissance man.

He would laugh at any macho male who suggested that his friendships with women made him less of a man – he knows that these friendships enrich his life, broaden his viewpoint, and stimulate his mind.

THE GOSSIP FACTOR

Yet society does do its best to make male-female friendships difficult to achieve and awkward to maintain. Ours is a suspicious, cynical, sex-oriented world where all touching is assumed to be a preliminary to sex. Even people who are enjoying a heterosexual friendship themselves look at a similar relationship between two other people and mutter, "There must be more to it than that."

In a way, I suppose that there is often a certain amount of sexual tension between a man and a woman, but it is immature to assume that such tension must automatically lead to sexual relations. Love, yes. All fully developed friendships contain an element of love that finds expression in concern, tenderness, empathy, caring. When the friends are of the opposite sex, the world does not understand, or want to believe, that these expressions of love are merely the natural outgrowth of friendship.

Consequently, male-female friendships are often misunderstood by the rest of the world. I have several male friends whom I love – but we are not lovers. There is a difference. It always saddens me when people don't recognize the possibility of that difference.

Some people might reply to that, "Surely what other people think doesn't matter!" I used to believe that when I was younger. Now I know that what other people think may not matter, but what they say can have an effect on people's lives.

Gossip can make a friendship seem tawdry. Even when a relationship shines with an exhilarating exchange of ideas, gossip can lessen its lustre. Where once openness was the rule, self-consciousness invades. Where once you accepted each other as people who shared certain interests and enjoyed each other's company, gossip makes you see each other differently. You become acutely conscious of the sexual possibilities. Once aware of the talk your friendship has stimulated, you start to behave differently in public. Before you know it, friendship is impossible. Sometimes you think, "Well, if I'm going to have the name, I might as well have the game," and you do become lovers. More often, you simply stop seeing each other.

Anne: "After I was divorced, I became acquainted again with a man I'd known when I was very young. He was also divorced. His life had contained an unusual amount of tragedy and he had made up his mind that he didn't want to get involved with anyone, let alone get married. I accepted that. He began taking me out to dinner about once a month and we found ourselves enjoying each other's company immensely. There was a lot of affection between us. Gradually, the word got around that we were seeing each other, and all kinds of pressure began to be put on us. People would ask us to dinner parties as a couple. They would make pointed remarks about our getting married. I could ignore it, but he couldn't. He was an old-fashioned, rather gallant sort of man and he decided that he was compromising me, that people would get the idea that I was his girl and he didn't want that. He didn't want me to be cut off from meeting other men and he didn't want the pressure of feeling that somehow, although he had never made a commitment himself, society had committed him. It was a beautiful friendship but gossip killed it."

Even if a man and a woman can withstand and dismiss the gossip and go on behaving naturally and normally, when there are others involved, the possibility of hurt has to be considered. The other woman in the man's life - or the other man in the woman's - may not be secure enough to laugh off knowing, suggestive, leering looks and comments.

Caroline: "I was one of those people who thought I was tough enough to be able to take gossip. I met a man through my work and I fell madly in love with his mind. We would have lunch once a week and talk and talk and talk. He never laid a hand on me and there wasn't a suggestion of our having an affair, but his companionship was so stimulating that I would be on a high from one encounter to the next. That went on for a year. I was naive and, I guess, selfish. I never even thought about what people might be saying - until I heard that his wife had gone into the hospital with severe depression. People couldn't wait to tell her about us. I stopped seeing him, but I resented having to give that friendship up. I thought about going to the wife, to try to explain, but I realized that for her, the humiliation that our casual friendship had caused was as real as the pain that might have come from an affair. If only we had once in awhile included her."

Sometimes the gossips are right. There may be an intense fantasy affair going on in the minds of both parties. The friends may never become physical lovers, but they are lovers nonetheless. In this case, a husband or wife may have good reason to be jealous – and helpless. It is harder to compete with an unrealized, romanticized fantasy than it is to confront a real – and therefore imperfect – rival.

HOMOSEXUAL FRIENDS

Many a woman can say without a trace of facetiousness, "Some of my best friends are homosexuals." The female-homosexual friendship has long been accepted in wealthy circles. The world's jet-set women are surrounded by homosexual men. Mrs. Rich includes them in exciting parties, invites them to visit her winter home, uses them as extra men at dinner, provides them with social access. In return, they take her dancing, escort her to opening nights, take an interest in her home and her clothes, and fill the spaces left by a husband who is usually absent. He may be absent through death or divorce, or because he is totally preoccupied with business, or because he is busy pursuing his own extramarital interests. If he is alive and still married, he is happy to pay the bills for his wife's homosexual friends because they keep her occupied, reduce the amount of nagging he might have to endure, and they are safe escorts.

The "safe" aspect of the homosexual creates an ambivalent response in women. On the one hand, more and more men are declaring themselves to be homosexuals; that can be discouraging, because it means there are fewer and fewer potential sexual partners for a woman. But any woman who has a homosexual friend can also admit that it is pure heaven to have a relationship with a man in which sex (how to get out of going to bed with him, how to make him want to go to bed if he isn't interested, and the countless other permutations that pervade other male-female relationships) is not an issue. On every other score, the homosexual is a marvellous date. He usually is an excellent dancer, someone who enjoys dancing for the sake of dancing, not just because it is a way to get close to his partner. He openly admires a woman's clothes, helps her choose them if she asks him, and he has no macho hang-ups about the ballet, the theatre, or art galleries.

He can be bitchy. This is especially true of older homosexuals who no longer can attract partners. The homosexual may also be possessive, taking every opportunity to let people know the extent of his influence over a woman, sulking if he is left out of a party, openly scornful of a woman's other friends.

He may steal a woman's husband. He may even fool her and turn out to be bisexual, intent on seducing both of them. All of those things have happened. But he may also turn out to be the very best friend, male or female, that a woman will ever have – loyal, understanding, caring, and wonderful company, because he sees a woman not as a sex object, but as a person.

JUST FRIENDS
Some women claim that their best friends are ex-lovers. That has not been the experience of the women in this book.

Anne: "I've tried to maintain a friendship with one or two of my ex-lovers, but it doesn't work. I shared a lot with one of them outside of our sexual relationship and for years we would get together every few months for lunch. But he seemed to find it necessary to prove that he could, if he wanted to, still get me into bed. And he did, not because I wanted to, but because I cared about his ego and I couldn't bring myself to say no. I began to find excuses to avoid our lunches and now we don't see each other at all. I'm sorry that the relationship moved to that stage, because now my memories of him are tinged with embarrassment.

"I was able to maintain one friendship, but I think we were always more friends than lovers. We only made love once, when we both happened to be in a strange city at the same time. We had dinner, and we ended up in bed together. I guess you could say we fell off the wagon. We never talked about it, but we never let it happen again. Mind you, the bed was terrific, but we knew it couldn't go anywhere. We were both married then and our spouses were friends. I guess unconsciously we both looked down the road and saw what would be ahead. I valued his friendship too much to risk it for a sexual liaison that could never be allowed to develop. I suppose he felt the same way.

"We still see each other regularly, but neither of us ever mentions our one night together. I would be curious to know what he remembers of it. I know that, in my mind, that brief sexual encounter has acquired a magic that I'm sure wasn't there."

Caroline: "I've tried to stay friends with some of my ex-lovers, but it has never worked. I was afraid to ask anything of them as a friend, for fear that they would think I was taking advantage of the intimacy we once knew. They seemed to find it hard to relax with me. I suspect that they think of me as some kind of ex-wife. I know too much about them to accept them as flawless. And I'm uncomfortable with my husband when those men are around. I'm terrified that some vibration might give away what was between us, and I wouldn't ever want to hurt my husband by confronting him with one of my ex-lovers. Or worse, by putting him in a situation where he accepted the guy and was nice to him, without knowing about us, while the guy would know and possibly feel smug about having cuckolded my husband."

Diane: "I can't be friends with my ex-lovers because the relationships ended on hysterical angry notes and some of that anger is still inside me. Besides, I've told my current man all about my other relationships, names, everything. So he knows who they are, what happened between us, how hurt I was. He would never understand a friendship."

Edna: "The divorced man I know suggested recently that perhaps we should be content to be friends only. I resented that, because it seemed to suggest that friendship was a second-best thing, something lower down the scale than a love affair. As far as I'm concerned, it takes the same kind of commitment to be a friend as it does to be a lover and I realize that what made my marriage so good was the friendship I knew with my husband. I would make the same demands on a friend – commitment, loyalty, love – that I would on a lover. But, while it isn't necessary for my friend to be my lover, unless a lover can also be a friend, the relationship won't last."

Frances: "Before I started my affair, I developed a close friendship with one of the men I work with at the office. We had similar situations, unhappy marriages in which we felt we were not valued sexually. Yet there was no physical attraction between us. One weekend when my husband was away, he came to see me. I was particularly depressed and upset. He held me in his arms and comforted me for hours. That non-sexual touching was very healing. Everyone should experience something like that. I think that it might be possible only between two people who haven't got something going sexually."

Affection is asexual. Until we recognize that, until we realize that the pats, the hugs, the hand-holding, and the kisses of friendship are non-sexual in their nature, then friendship - not only between men and women, but also between men and men, and between women and women - will, sadly, be suspect.

CHAPTER 6

Men As Seducers

"Life is a tragedy for those who feel, and a comedy for those who think."

La Bruyère

All men are not "after only one thing." But those who are on the sexual prowl are so obvious and so blatant in their approach that a woman can be forgiven for sometimes concluding that, in this way, all men are alike.

Yet even when they are searching for sexual action, they are not alike. They differ, for one thing, in confidence. There are some men who seem to have no doubts at all about their desirability. It never occurs to them that a woman might not want them – they assume that every female from twelve to 112 is not only available, but longing to go to bed with them. Sadly, it never occurs to these men that a woman might see something more valuable in them than stud service. Nor do they realize how sick they sound as they litter every conversation with the names of women who, in these men's imaginations, are chasing them.

Some psychologists contend that men with apparently

boundless egos are really so insecure and uncertain of their masculinity that they must constantly make conquests in order to prove their virility to themselves. Traditional women, indoctrinated in the belief that men do indeed have fragile egos, have tended to encourage these men, rather than hurt their feelings. Whenever a woman does try to make it clear that she is not sexually interested, she has trouble convincing such a man. Since he values himself only as a sexual machine, he is threatened by sexual rejection. If she persists in saying no, he usually turns on her, accusing her of being lesbian, frigid, unfeminine. Why else would she resist him?

These men brag.

One such man made it a point to tell me at a cocktail party that he had been to bed with every woman in that very crowded room, except me. Later, when he pursued me (not because he wanted me but because he wanted a perfect record), he finally demanded, "Look, I know you want me. Why play games? Why won't you go to bed with me?"

It was, I thought, a moment for truth.

"Of course I find you attractive. But that's not enough. It may come as a shock to you, but it is just as easy today for a woman as it is for a man to have a different bed partner every night. She does not have to be beautiful - just available. I choose not to do that, for many reasons, including the fact that it would offend my sense of fastidiousness. But if I am going to have sex with you, since you sleep with everyone I might as well sleep around, too. There would certainly be no point in my being fastidious. There are women in this room I wouldn't have lunch with - yet you are suggesting that I knowingly share a bed partner with them. No, thank you."

He gave up on me. Not because he was discouraged, or because he understood what I meant. No, he gave up on me, he told anyone who would listen, because I was too demanding, too possessive.

Caroline talks of a man she dated for a few months after her divorce. She liked him, they shared many interests, and they were happy together. But every time he met one of her friends, he would declare later that the woman had made a pass at him. Twice, Caroline believed him and found herself being cool to old and valued friends.

But when a pattern began to emerge, she became skeptical. Even if it were true, even if all her friends were after her man, she wondered why he insisted on telling her. Then he said that her daughter was sexually interested in him.

Caroline: "I was very upset. I knew my daughter liked him and I was glad of that. Certainly I was aware that there was the normal male-female tension or flirtation in their relationship, but that didn't bother me. She had been without a father for two years and I was pleased that there was an adult male who would flirt with her, to confirm her femininity and serve as a practising ground for her own dating life.

"But I was not competitive with her, nor was she with me. Whatever attraction she felt for him was not important until he made it important. I stopped seeing him. No doubt he thinks it was because I was jealous. But it was because I was disgusted that he wasn't mature enough to handle my daughter's feelings in a positive way."

There are other men who, although they are not particularly confident, are optimists. These men operate on the Fuller-Brush system: knock on enough doors and eventually they make a sale. They try with everybody. It doesn't matter whether the woman is old, young, virgin, experienced, bright, dumb, single, married, ugly, or attractive. What counts is that she might say yes. It is called – for reasons that elude me – "getting lucky."

TECHNICAL DATA
Although these men have the same destination in mind, they choose different routes to reach it. The most popular method is an appeal to a woman's sympathy, arousing in her either maternal or Florence Nightingale instincts. Others try to make a woman feel responsible for them, while some men try a sophisticated, man-of-the-world approach. The most contemporary technique may be response to the tendency of some feminists to openly evaluate and criticize men. It is aggressive, rooted in insult, and designed to put a woman on the defensive.

Aggressive Albert, for example, walked up to me in the middle of a dinner party and, without any preamble or apparent cause, said, "What you need, lady, is to have a man land on you like a two-ton truck." Had the method worked, I would have spent the rest of the night pursuing him, asking him what he meant. Instead, I merely shrugged and asked, "Again?"

He has a less subtle cousin, *Chauvinist Carl*, who considers himself an expert on women and what ails them. "Lady," he says (and we wonder why the word lady has fallen into disrepute!), "what you need is a good fuck." To which a quick-witted feminist once replied, "Yes, indeed. What you don't realize, sir, is how hard it is to get a good one."

Far more common is *Samaritan Sam*. He is ready to service every separated, divorced, or widowed woman on the basis of need. "You've had a man, so you're used to sex. It must be awful for you to go without. Count on me. I'll drop by for twenty minutes on my way home from work." Sam is so confident of the urgency of the newly single woman's need that he sometimes doesn't even announce himself. He just arrives.

Detached David is a really modern man, the honest type. After you have made love for the first time, he tells you he doesn't want to get involved. Into your bed and into your body, yes, but involved, no.

Lonely Larry longs to find the perfect relationship. All he has ever wanted in life is one perfect woman who will be mate, companion, lover. But, alas, he has never been lucky in love. You could be his rabbit's foot – or his cat's paw.

Mannie from Missouri asks you to prove yourself. "I guess you're not interested in sex anymore. Women like you are too success-oriented to be sexy. Of course, if you were a real woman..."

Challenging Charlie attacks. "And you call yourself a liberated woman...boy, have you got hang-ups." Someone should tell Charlie that liberation gave women, above all, the right to say no.

Egotistical Edward can only explain away a rebuff by defining a fault in the woman. "Obviously you're (check one) frigid, lesbian..."

If all these techniques fail, any one of these men can turn into *Maniac Martin*. His method is simple: rape. He doesn't call it that because he thinks when a woman says no she's just being coy; she really means yes. Maniac Martin is often a friend or a friend of a friend. He agrees to pick you up or take you home, or gets into your apartment by offering to give you some legal, tax, or plumbing advice. Having been invited in, he is sure that you will never complain to anyone, so the battle is on.

While most intelligent women can see through the aggressive approaches, few can resist an appeal to their sympathy. The classic "My-wife-doesn't-understand-me" line is still very much in use. *Harried Harry* gives that opener a modern twist as he tells a female coworker a long sad story about what a terrible housekeeper his wife is. Why, he hasn't had a decent home-cooked meal in years.

Deprived Dick confides even more intimate details. His wife is frigid, she hasn't been to bed with him in months. Or she's an invalid or a mental case. Better still, she's untrustworthy, a poor mother, promiscuous, or having an affair with his best friend. Not only has Dick been deprived of sex, but his confidence needs a boost. What woman could resist?

Pained Peter has other problems. No one has ever loved him. He is facing his fiftieth birthday and is convinced that he is over the hill and life has passed him by. Many Pained Peters are men with drinking problems, and there are still many women ready to believe that alcoholism can be cured by the love of a good woman.

Wounded Willie has horrible tales to tell of how badly women have treated him. "All women are alike," he says, confident that the listener will try to prove him wrong and thereby make up for the wickedness of her sisters.

Juvenile Joe is an appealing, perpetual little boy. He calls his wife Mother, wears socks that don't match and a tie that is soiled. He can't and won't leave Mother, but he would like to find a woman willing to be a wetnurse.

Humbled Herbert has the advantage of a little honesty. He's the man who tells you he isn't good enough for you. Unfortunately, few women believe him in time.

Tricky Tom presents a woman with her greatest challenge. Late at night after a wine-soaked dinner, he cries real tears and tells her, "I'm impotent."

Teenage boys have often tried to make girls feel responsible for their erections. There are still some adult males using that approach. There are the "Let-me-put-it-in-just-an-inch" fellows or, worse, the ones who promise not to penetrate. "Just let me rub it against you." Or even more misleading, "Just let me lie beside you and give you a cuddle."

More sophisticated versions of this shift-of-responsibility technique emphasize the emotional instead of the physical need. "My work is suffering.... I can't sleep.... I don't want to live without you." Since few women can resist either a man with tears in his eyes or the chance to play such an important role in another's life, it is not surprising that this approach often succeeds.

Men of the world make women feel that they have something rare and unusual to offer. This approach can be as earthy as that of *Stud Steve*, who has, according to him, the largest penis, the longest staying power, and the most imaginative technique in the world. Or it can be as smooth as that of *Expensive Edgar*, who showers a woman with perfume, flowers, jewelry, books of poetry, and ever-so-subtle suggestions about a future together. "Someday, when I show you the Taj Mahal..."

Cool Claude appeals to a woman's sophistication: "My wife and I have an understanding." The tone of voice makes it clear that only an unsophisticated square would be unwilling to become part of their understanding.

Heroic Humphrey is always facing a crisis, danger, or the unknown. He is flying off to interview Idi Amin; being transferred to Iran; going to war; having chest pains; suffering from a rare and incurable disease; on the verge of a breakdown. It is imperative that he make the most of every moment.

Shocking Simon says outrageous things. He is very often an older man, wealthy and respected in the community, with an admired wife. He chooses his moments with great care. Put him in a social situation where he is sure a woman will be too embarrassed to make a fuss, and he acts out his fantasies verbally. At a reception for an ambassador, Shocking Simon may well turn to the woman on his right and ask, "Do you perform fellatio?" (Probably his choice of words would be much more crude.)

Safe Sandy advertises. He wears a tie with a vasectomy symbol printed on it and, just in case you don't recognize that, tells you the details of the operation.

THE EXCEPTIONS

At the other end of the scale, there are some men who really bewilder women. These are the men with no confidence at all. They enjoy sex and are heterosexual, but it never occurs to them that a woman is interested in them. They don't know how to approach a woman, send a signal, or read one if it comes their way. With this kind of man, a woman must be the aggressor and she cannot afford to be too subtle. If she undresses in front of him, his first thought will be that the room is too hot.

Men differ not only in confidence and approach, but in motive. Some men – fewer than women realize – simply want sexual relief. It doesn't matter to them who the woman is, what kind of person she might be, or what she looks like. To this man in this mood, she is a convenience. There are other men who find sex an outlet for tension, vengeance, aggression, or hostility. And there are some men who consider sex just another aspect of competition; this type of man might make a pass at a woman because he wants to score against her husband.

The best men (from a woman's point of view) are the ones who are searching not only for sexual satisfaction but also for human contact, for an interruption of loneliness, and for intimacy. Today these men don't expect every encounter to result in a long-lasting relationship, but they reject any experience that is certain to diminish either party. They wait for a response to their signal or an invitation before they assume that there will be sex. They are both discreet and responsible.

They have an old-fashioned label: they are called gentlemen.

CHAPTER 7

Men As Lovers

"After all, the world is but an amusing theater, and I see no reason why a pretty woman should not play a principal part in it."

Countess du Barry

In their book, *The Pleasure Bond*, Masters and Johnson say that sexual relationships mirror personal relationships: "Since emotionally stable human beings are not split personalities, how they feel about each other and how they act toward each other is essentially no different at night from what it is by day." That explains the wide range of feelings that a man and a woman can share in bed, be it with mutually exclusive partners in a long-lasting relationship, or with many partners.

The women interviewed for this book speak about variety, not only in their own levels of satisfaction but also in the sexual techniques and responses of their partners. Undoubtedly, the needs and the moods of the women influenced the quality of each encounter; but their recollections underline how varied men are - even, or perhaps especially, in bed.

Anne: "Men are definitely not the same in bed. Every man I've ever slept with has had some idiosyncracy that was his own.

"There was one who asked, 'What's my name?' just before he came to orgasm and another who asked, 'Who do you belong to?'

"There was one who always prayed after sex. I never did figure out whether he was praying for forgiveness or the strength to do it again. There was another who would never come inside me. His grandfather had gotten some girl pregnant and the cost to the family was so enormous that he took no chances. He put it rather quaintly: he only planted seed in his wife. There was even one who wanted to dress up in my underwear and high-heeled shoes; but that was too kinky, even for me.

"Almost every man I've ever met has made it clear that he considered himself to be a fantastic lover. Some of them would start out fantastic, but after the third time, when they were sure that they had me, they would become lazy. I have memories of a lot of men taking off their clothes, stretching out, and then leaving the rest to me. Since I am not a prostitute, it is not surprising that I sometimes resent that.

"Men are most different in their attitude to oral sex. Almost all of them like it to be done to them, but many don't want to do it to a woman. I think there are a lot of men who really don't like women and this is where it shows. If a man doesn't like the way a woman smells (and I don't mean her body odour, I mean the smell of a woman), or if he finds her body repugnant except as a receptacle, oral sex is an impossibility. Some men do it because they think it's their duty. You can almost hear them thinking, 'Now I'll spend thirty seconds down there and get it over with.' I'd rather they didn't bother. Others do it at the beginning of an affair, but once they feel they can take you for granted, they forget about it.

"Some men are totally predictable. You know they are

going to come into your bed, rotate your right breast, then your left, and in two minutes it's all over.

"Some men can only come when they are on top. They'll let you be astride for a while, but they can't ejaculate until they're riding you. I knew one who could only come when he entered me from the back.

"There was another one who took great pride in the length of time he could maintain an erection. That's okay, up to a point, but when it goes on for hours and hours, it's exhausting. You get so you just want it to come to an end, to be left alone. It's also unsatisfying. Sure, I may have had several orgasms, but I am not happy because I haven't given pleasure. Or so it seems.

"There's a feeling too with some men that their orgasm is always a very solitary thing. They satisfy you first, then they look after themselves in such a way that suggests you're not there.

"Most men just assume that sex has been great for me. But few of them ever ask me how it was, and a lot of the time it wasn't very good. Two men were really memorable lovers and I will always feel close to them, be willing to do anything for them. The first one was a very inexperienced man who started out with a pathetic erection. The first time we made love, he came as soon as he entered me. But he cared about me and he wanted me to be satisfied, so after that, he would spend a lot of time making love before penetrating me. Of all the men I've known, this one enjoyed touching the most. He loved to caress me and he enjoyed being caressed. He always brought me to orgasm with oral sex or manually first, so I was never unsatisfied. As experienced as I was, I found it hard to relax, to spend so long in what I thought of as teenage petting, and I would urge him to come inside me. But he would insist on taking his time. By the end of a year, I was his slave and he was a very different partner. He not only had full erections, but total control.

"The other man was high-spirited, energetic, and

exciting. He was mentally stimulating and sex with him was always a surprise - bathtubs, showers, in front of a fire, airplanes, on a picnic. Tender, wild, oral sex, anal sex, spankings - he lived out my fantasies.

"You just know that some men like to make love. They like the contact, the communication part of it. Others are just interested in coming. But when I compare men this way, I find I am not comparing their technique so much as how I felt when sex was over.

"For me, the period after sex is very important. There was a popular song about that a little while ago, something about still loving you after the loving. I don't mind if a man goes to sleep, so long as he goes to sleep with me. All he has to do is put an arm around me, cuddle me, even let a foot touch mine. When he rolls away abruptly, it's as though he's saying, 'I've used you. I'm finished with you.' I feel lonely with a man like that.

"But what really turns me off is the man who leaps out of bed to scrub himself. That makes me feel terrible. There are so many loving ways to do that. The two men I will always remember were really good at that. I remember as much about our showers and baths together as I do about our lovemaking. And that loving washing up of each other usually led to another, tenderer lovemaking.

"My ex-husband taught me my most important lesson about men and, at the same time, he helped me to discover something about myself. After our separation, we would see each other occasionally, and inevitably we would have sex. That period was very stormy; we had some of our most open quarrels after our marriage broke up. It was painful, but I learned a lot. I remember saying once that it was obvious he still had desire for me, since we always had sex. He told me then that it was quite possible for him to want to have intercourse with me, to be aroused to an erection, and go through the whole sex act without experiencing any pleasure because the feelings he had for me were not conducive to pleasure. That was when I realized that, for all my experience, I had shortchanged men's emotional needs. Why should a woman think that a man is any different? Why should we assume that sex, removed from caring, means any more to a man than it does to a woman? I have not made that mistake again."

Frances: "I was really in love with my husband when we married and I think I am a sexy woman. I know I am a sexy woman. But I got so I couldn't stand sex with him because it was always the same.

"He would come home and sometimes not say a word to me all evening. Certainly there was never any build-up to sex. He wouldn't flirt with me during the evening or ask me to dance or stop by my chair to touch me. At eleven o'clock he'd go to bed. If he wasn't in the mood, he'd go right to sleep. If he was, he'd roll over and take me. Always in the same position. In the same way. He'd rub my right breast, never the left, and never gently, always more pinching than rubbing. It was so predictable I wanted to scream. In, and over. Then up he'd jump for a shower before he went to sleep.

"We couldn't talk about it. I suggested a marriage counsellor, but he said I was crazy, there was nothing wrong.

"So I'm having an affair. My husband still makes love to me now and then but it means nothing. With my boss, I've discovered that the kind of sexy loving that I dreamed about is possible. I realize that the fact that our relationship is clandestine is part of the excitement. We can't be together that often, so there is always a big build-up. And we share a lot of things because we work together. But it's more than that. I feel important to him. In bed, sex is always different. He has explored every part of me. There is a suggestion of violence. He doesn't really hurt me, but he does make me feel submissive and

I find that very sexy. I would do anything my lover asked me to do, and I find myself hoping that he will ask me to do something I haven't even imagined. I love to dress up for him in garter belts and sexy underwear, or just wear gloves and stockings, anything to add to the excitement. To my amazement, I don't feel embarrassed or inhibited."

Edna: "I never really thought about sex while my husband was alive. I was a virgin when I was married, and so was he, and we were pretty fumbly about things. I was very happy with him and it never occurred to me that I would spend a large part of my life without him. If what I hear and read is typical of what goes on with most couples, then I guess we weren't very adventurous. I wonder now if he was disappointed, if I should have been sexier, but I always enjoyed our lovemaking. I guess it's a funny word to use, but it was very comfortable.

"I actually had my first orgasm while I was nursing my first child. I never told my husband that, and I don't suppose I'll ever tell my son. After that, I was a little hungrier for sex, but then we had the kids and there never was much privacy. When we went away on a vacation together, which only happened three times, we would scrub each other's backs and have sex a little more often, but we still didn't try anything very fancy.

"I realize now that I was very protected, but that's not a word I would have used before my husband died. It took the past year to show me that. I can't believe the way some of the men I've known for years behave all of a sudden – finding an excuse to rub my breast when they're helping me with a coat, grabbing me in the kitchen for an open-mouthed kiss.

"My friends have stopped asking me to their homes for dinner because they don't know what to do with an unattached woman. Or they put pressure on me to dig up a date. I resent the suggestion that I'm a better guest with a man along, even if he's a bore or a drunk. But I don't really mind not being invited out like that because I was finding it hard to know how to behave with a friend whose husband was grabbing me under the bridge table. Why, one of them even undid his fly and started waving his penis at me in an elevator. The old fool. I'm lonely, but it's for the love and companionship I knew with my husband, not for a penis. It was certainly a shock to me to discover that every man who took me out expected me to be not only willing but anxious to make love to him.

"I have two regular dates, and I guess that makes me rather lucky since a lot of women my age have no one. One of them, the divorced one, will soon leave the scene I think, because he thinks bed should be automatic. He keeps telling me he just wants to have a good time, not get involved, whatever that means. I wouldn't want to be a friend to a man who couldn't be involved with me, let alone have sex with him. And I don't think I should have to pay for my dinner with sex. The other man, the widower, is a little more considerate, perhaps because our circumstances are similar. We cuddle each other a lot, kiss, hold hands, touch each other, but he doesn't put pressure on me and I appreciate that. I don't want to be alone for the rest of my life, but I'm afraid. I'm afraid, still, to have sex when I am not married. What if he disappears from my life then? What if he doesn't like my body? I don't think I could handle it if I didn't hear from him again, if something went wrong. It's not easy, courting again, when you thought you were safely rescued from that."

Diane: "I am not sure that I have really had an orgasm, not even yet. The earth hasn't moved or anything. But I have had good sex and bad sex.

"When it's bad I feel as though my partner is just masturbating inside me. I don't think it matters then whether it's with me or someone else. Bad sex makes me feel cheap, used. I don't mind acting out the part of a whore, but I don't want to be treated like a whore.

"When sex is good, there's a feeling of intimacy, and for me that comes from talking. I am really turned on by a man who talks to me, not just before sex, but during and after. When I know that what I am doing is pleasing him, I just want to please him more and more. And it's not so important that I have an orgasm, as long as the sex is loving. It really matters to me to have a man spend the night with me. I like it when a man wants to sleep with me, wake up with me. And morning sex is always the best. If he does have to get up and go home before morning, then I want him to phone me when he wakes up. The guy who doesn't phone me until he wants sex again is not for me.

"I've had one experience with a man who came into my life, made a big impact on me, seemed to want and to promise intimacy, took me to bed, and then disappeared. No phone call, no nothing. I think that's the worst. You wonder and you wonder, always, what was wrong with you. Does it ever occur to a woman that there could be something wrong with the man? I still think about him sometimes and wonder, 'What did I do wrong?'"

Caroline: "There was a time when I could separate sex and love. I slept with a number of different men and there was never any emotion involved. I was horny; he was there. Sometimes it was great, sometimes it wasn't. The worst part was afterwards. Before, you're in this big fever, and you tear off your clothes and fall on each other. But when it's over, you realize you have nothing to say, or you might not like each other, or one of you says the wrong thing, and the mood is dead. I used to wish that there was some way to vanish at the end of sex like that, without that awful silence and the urge to fill it with anything, anything.

"I had a lot of good sex and a lot of bad sex in those days.

The worst were the guys who were in love with their penises. They'd admire them and I was supposed to admire them, to assure them I had seen nothing like theirs. That was the basis of their whole ability to make love. Now I know that the size of a man's penis is not supposed to matter and that, with imagination, you can compensate, because it doesn't matter. But I do want to say that there is something very erotic about a really big penis, and in the initial stages of an affair a large penis can be enough. But eventually, the man has to be able to do a few things, or it all gets boring.

"I think men should pay more attention to their underwear. I remember one short man I was really attracted to. I was so anxious to make love to him – until he took off his clothes and was standing there in boxer shorts that came down to his knees. It was so comic that I couldn't feel sexy.

"First times are terrible. A couple have to know each other to make love well. Up to a point, familiarity is essential if you want to be really sensuous.

"My second husband is the best lover I have ever known. He loves my body, he likes to watch me walk around without clothes, and he tells me that I please him. He is never in a hurry about sex. In fact, a lot of the time, I hurry him. I suppose the familiarity of marriage kills sex for some people, but it has given us the chance to find out what we like, as well as to feel safe enough and have time enough to try different things.

"Some of it is knowing how lucky I am. I had gotten to the point where I hated casual sex, was afraid of what might happen to me. And I've had enough experience to know that a man who really likes to make love is a find. I think our fidelity to each other has helped build the intensity of what we share. And I value it. I won't let anything come in the way of the time we spend together."

Bettina: "All the men I've known have had some kind

of power - wealth, corporate position, political power, social power. And they were alike in that they played the power game even in their personal relationships. Loving this kind of man is like playing chess: you have to understand strategy and you must always play the game.

"These men fall into two types. One isn't interested in having to work at a relationship with a woman. He wants that part of his life to be easy. His business life has enough crises, enough problems to solve. He won't put any energy into his love life. He doesn't want to talk to his woman or share his life with her. He just wants her to be available. He seeks out a woman who can be satisfied with material things. Above all, she must be easy to satisfy in bed. He wants her to have an orgasm ready to go off like a doorbell, because he will not spend time in bed with her. He usually picks the dumb, pretty girls whose demands are met - temporarily, at least - with a cheque or a present.

"The other type, the ones I married, want a woman to be a sort of sexual Mount Everest. This man won't turn down easy sex, but he marries the woman who is not just hard to get, but hard to please. He needs a sense of achievement, even in bed. He doesn't ever want to be able to take a woman for granted. When he does, that's the end of the relationship for him; he's bored. He expects a woman to play games with him. He responds to that.

"Without exception, powerful men bring the telephone into the bedroom. I've had a man undress me and fondle my breasts while he was selling a football team on the phone. I've performed fellatio while a man talked to his secretary. And I knew one man who rolled away after sex, not to go to sleep, but to make a phone call.

"Powerful men take pride in their skills, so they are usually technically good lovers. But some of them are always remote, detached, cold. They allow no one, not even a wife, to be intimate with them. With this kind of man, there's a terrible emptiness after sex. The warmth of being together is ended so quickly.

"Others are compartmentalized. They can create a feeling of great intimacy, but when they walk out the door, they forget about a woman until their need for sex becomes so urgent that they have to put business aside.

"These men are used to writing the rules, so they expect to call the shots in a relationship. They use their money to hold you. If you're depressed, take a trip. If you feel neglected, here's a diamond bracelet. They'll give you anything, except some part of themselves. And sometimes they'll give you anything except cash. One of my husbands would let me charge anything, anywhere in the world. But I never had a dollar in my wallet. He seemed to think that if he couldn't hold me with his penis, he would do it by money, by making me dependent.

"Powerful men are unlikely to admit that they need anyone because that gives that person power over them. They almost always have incredible energy. Sometimes they pour that into their work and seem to have little need for, or interest in, sex. But others are always interested in sex, always having affairs, sometimes several at once.

"The only man I ever loved was married to me, carrying on an active social and sex life with me, running a huge business, and was chairman of a national charity drive. And he had two full-time mistresses, each of whom he saw three times a week. Plus God knows how many one-night stands when he travelled.

"The best lover I ever had was the oldest. He was past the stage of competition and I was his retirement plan. What he lacked in stamina, he made up for in tenderness. I suppose he might have complained that he didn't have as many erections and orgasms as he did when he was a young man, but I had more orgasms with him than with all my other husbands put together. And because he truly cherished me, I found myself being tender and caring. That relationship brought me more peace, more pleasure than any other."

CHAPTER 8

Men As Husbands

"It is as absurd to say that a man can't love one woman all his life as it is to say that a violinist needs several violins to play the same piece of music."

Honoré de Balzac

There are many kinds of husbands. There are those who are really fathers to their wives, and some who are really sons. There are men who are househusbands for women who work - men who are skilled at shopping, cleaning, and cooking - and there are those who would never help around the house, whether they are the financial providers or not. There are husbands who see marriage in black and white - he puts out the garbage, she cooks, he can play around, but she can't. And there are husbands who are husbands in name only; in behaviour they are still bachelors. There are husbands who never talk, and some who never listen. There are husbands who believe that their only function is to pay the bills; and some wonderful ones who want to be full partners, sharing and growing in mutual commitment to a relationship that they value, respect, and want to maintain.

THE PSYCHOLOGY OF
THE EXTRAMARITAL AFFAIR

Not all husbands play around – but half do.

At least that's the conclusion of an American study conducted by Dr. Antony Pietropinto and Jacqueline Simmenauer for their book, *Beyond the Male Myth*. There are moments in a single woman's life when she could challenge the results of both those surveys, moments when she is convinced that every married man she meets is having, looking for, or fantasizing about an extramarital affair.

The motives are many. Sometimes there is a wife who is no longer attractive, no longer interested in sex, or disinterested in what her husband does, as long as he continues to pay the bills. This man is genuinely lonely, looking for a companion as much as for sex.

Sometimes, the man's search for extramarital sex is prompted by fear. He may be afraid of getting old: the best of life seems to be going by too quickly and he is missing out. This anxiety may be complicated by a sudden realization that all the things that he has valued – the success he has coveted, the material things he has worked for – really mean nothing. His life seems to have been wasted.

Just as often, the need for an affair is rooted in boredom, an expression of the emotion described by Simone de Beauvoir in *The Second Sex*:

> Eroticism is a movement toward the Other, this is its essential character; but in the deep intimacy of the couple, husband and wife become for one another the Same; no exchange is any longer possible between them, no giving and no conquering. Thus if they do continue to make love, it is often with a sense of shame: they feel that the sexual act is no longer an intersubjective experience in which each goes beyond self, but rather a kind of joint masturbation.

There are times in a man's life when he thinks he needs to feel the texture of a strange skin, to discover a new response, in order to reassure himself that he is still sexually attractive, in order to experience maximum sexual excitement. But beyond the need for a partner who is different, there is the need for a partner who will see him differently, a woman who does not remember him when he was a nobody, a woman who does not know about his weaknesses and his failures, a woman who can accept him as the person he is now, today, without any knowledge of all that went before. She is his clean slate.

Propinquity makes many affairs possible. Spending day after day in the company of an attractive woman who shares his problems, understands his work, has a part in his defeats and his triumphs, can lead to a desire for physical intimacy. If that doesn't happen at work, it can happen to any two people who share an intense cause, which is why political parties have always been fertile ground for extramarital affairs.

It is easy for couples in this situation to find time to be together. The after-work meeting has credibility, and if there is a sofa in the office, they have not only solved the problem of where, but they have added piquancy to the daytime hours when they must sit on that same sofa in front of others, sticking to business. In many cases, they are able to arrange out-of-town trips and so satisfy their lover's urge to sleep together.

A few - very few - unfaithful husbands take a sophisticated approach to extramarital sex. These are the men who are realistic about their needs and very practical about satisfying them. It is clearly understood from the start that they have no intention of ending their marriage, and this husband does nothing that will ever embarrass his wife. He provides for his extramarital affairs a conducive setting, one that assures both privacy and dignity, and he finds a woman who will be both exciting and discreet. Sometimes, he arranges for an apartment that is used exclusively for their assignation. Sometimes, if she is single, they use her apartment. He will insist that it be one with proper security and he may or may not pay the rent, as well as the rest of her bills. He recognizes that he cannot give this woman many things that will be important to her - he will never spend Christmas or his birthday with her, and he cannot take her out publicly. He makes up for it in other ways. He never lets the relationship seem cheap, makes it clear that he values the woman as a person and accepts responsibility for her emotions - up to a point. That point is his wife, who comes first.

Sometimes the responsibility becomes heavy and after a few years these men may discover that a mistress' demands can be as strident as a wife's, that the ritual of an affair can become as suffocating and monotonous as that of marriage. Then the affair ends, and is usually quickly replaced by another.

Other husbands are Summer Bachelors. They are model husbands from September until June, but once the kids and the wife are packed off to the cottage, a new life begins. They may take up with a pretty woman from the office; they may engage in a series of one-night stands with women met in bars; they may have a brief affair with a neighbour. They think nothing of using the marital bed for these liaisons. On the contrary, having the house at their disposal is essential. Most of the time, they haven't enough money to pay for a hotel or an apartment. In the autumn, when their wives return, they become model husbands again, with a fresh supply of fantasies to carry them through the winter months. When they make love to their wives, they can close their eyes and recreate other women and other moments.

Since Where to Do It and How to Do It without Getting Caught are the main things that worry a wandering husband, sometimes two or three of them get together to rent an apartment. This is usually in a slightly sleazy district, where they are unlikely to meet anyone they know. If they do, they can wink and assume that their acquaintances are there for the same reason. Initially, these men use the apartment one at a time, but after a while they begin to have group parties and sometimes end up sharing each other's women. The women are usually professional or semi-professional and there is a tacit understanding that in exchange for gifts and/or money, they will not talk.

Some husbands operate on the philosophy that if they sleep with each woman only once, it doesn't count. They take advantage of every opportunity, whether it's at work or while travelling. The place is never a problem. They've been known to make love in the linen closet at the Toronto General Hospital; in the stock rooms of the fabric department at Eaton's, in between floors in a stopped elevator on Bay Street; on a fire escape overlooking a seldom-used lane behind a hotel; on a back-stair landing at the office. They are expert at quickies. They know the name of every inexpensive hotel within forty miles. They are on friendly terms with every bellman and every *maître d'*, and don't hesitate to ask them to supply women. They have, and share with each other, a list of cheaters' restaurants, where it is understood that no one ever takes a wife.

Many of the married men who want to play around are so nervous about being caught that they develop elaborate James-Bond-type games. Last year, for example, a married man asked me to lunch. We set a day and agreed he would call me at the office to say where. When the day arrived, I was busy with a number of meetings. I told my secretary to hold all my calls, except the one from Mr. X. Twelve o'clock came and there was no message. One o'clock. Two o'clock. Finally, I assumed that something had gone wrong. I bought a sandwich in the cafeteria and ate at my desk.

That evening, he called me at home. "Where were

you?" he said. "I called and called and couldn't get through." I told him that that was impossible; I had left word that I was expecting his call and had checked several times for a message.

"Oh," he said, "I didn't leave my name. I left Edgar Bronfman's."

"Edgar Bronfman?" I was incredulous. "Why would you do that and why would you think that I would connect that with you?"

He left Edgar Bronfman's name because in Peter Newman's book, *The Bronfman Dynasty*, Edgar is quoted as telling Sam Bronfman, "It doesn't cost forty million dollars to get laid."

Since it would not be unusual for me in my work to get a call from a prominent businessman - even a Bronfman - I never connected the message my secretary had taken, several times, with this man. The subtlety escaped me. The crudity, when it was explained to me, killed any desire on my part to have anything to do with him, even to have lunch.

THE OTHER WOMAN'S STORY

Anne: "Some men are very naive about women. When I was on a winter vacation, as a houseguest of friends, I went to a very large dinner party. My dinner partner was an attractive man and we spent a pleasant two hours chatting. I did not make any sexual advances towards this man, so I was very surprised when later a maid came to tell me that he was at our front door. Terrified that my host would be awakened, I went to the door in my bathrobe, and was disconcerted to find that he expected me to let him into my bedroom.

"'I can't do that,' I said, 'I am a houseguest. Besides, I don't want to and I can't imagine why you would think I would let you.'

"He didn't hear that, or chose not to hear it. Instead, he sulked, put on his very best four-year-old's expression, and said, 'But you have to let me in. What would I tell my wife? I told her I was going out to play poker with the boys. I can't go home now.'"

Most married men just want to play; however boring their marriages might be, they don't want out of them. On the contrary, marriage provides them with a marvellous excuse to have sex without commitment. They build an elaborate story about the responsibilities they have, what wonderful mothers their wives are, how dependent their wives are, how they could never, ever leave their spouses, even though these women are frigid and all sex between them has been dead for years. (Violins, please.) This is told to a mistress while she is in her lover's arms. While she is enjoying his infidelity she is also supposed to be admiring his deep sense of responsibility.

Anne: "I can remember two very funny (in the bittersweet sense of that word) moments with a married man with whom I had an affair. One day, after sex, we were enjoying a glass of wine and talking. He was completely naked, propped on one elbow, with his other hand stroking my breast, when he said,'I would never do anything to hurt my wife.' I didn't know whether to laugh or cry at the irony of the situation, as well as at his capacity for self-deception.

"There was another time with the same man. We met at four o'clock in a downtown hotel. I got there first and ordered white wine and smoked salmon. We had a particularly beautiful time together and I didn't want him to leave. I asked him to spend the evening with me. 'I can't,' he said. 'I have to go home. We have a new maid and it's her first night.'"

Caroline: "One of my affairs was with a married man who shared everything with me. We went out to the best restaurants. He didn't seem to mind if people saw him with me. We took trips together and when his wife was away, he'd take me to their house. I'd cook his dinner, we'd make love. I danced nude for him in the living room, and we'd spend the night in the master bedroom. The relationship lasted three years. But he would never tell me he loved me. He'd tell me he felt something for me. But the word 'love' he reserved for his wife."

THE WIVES - THEIRS AND OTHER PEOPLES'

For some men, marriage is a way to have their cake and eat it too. These men resist divorce. They may leave their wives, or their wives may leave them, but there is a constant round of reconciliations. No matter how many affairs he has had, he drags his heels all the way to the divorce court. Out there, waiting, are all the women whom he told, "I'd marry you in a minute, but my wife won't give me a divorce." If the divorce goes through and he has to live up to those words, he'll be arrested for bigamy.

Often, a man's marriage break-up costs him a lot of money. In the aftermath, facing years of child support and two residences to maintain, he vows he will never get married again. But he needs - and finds - a woman. Sometimes she lives with him and has regular sex with him. Eventually, she wants to get married, and she rages at his wife's selfish refusal to give him a divorce. But he has never asked for one and usually stalls her attempts to get one, because he doesn't want to be free to marry again.

Canny married men play with married women only. One of the town's busiest and most successful philanderers told me, "Never play with anyone who doesn't have as much to lose as you do." Any married woman who has suddenly become single is familiar with the followers of this philosophy. Once, they were constantly on the phone, isolating her at parties, seeking out opportunities for sexual encounters. But the moment the woman is separated, these men disappear over her horizon, faster than a speeding bullet. Suddenly she represents the possibility of an involvement. And involvement, to these men, is a dirty word. They were only kidding.

Anne: "Through my affairs, I have seen the man's side of marriage. I realize that there is no such thing as one definitive truth in any relationship. It seems to me that many men and women don't value their marriages. They don't work at them. They let the romance die. I suppose I did that in my own marriage. Well, it's unlikely that I would ever get married again, but if I did, I would spend some of my time as a wife pretending that I was a mistress. Many men have very unsatisfactory sex lives. Women don't realize that the fact that a man has an erection doesn't mean that he wants to be satisfied right away. There's often a lag between the physical and mental in a man, and a man has to be mentally aroused before he can really enjoy sex. He appreciates a woman who can help him pace his sexual drive so that he can get the maximum pleasure from it."

Edna: "My husband was one of the 50 per cent who are faithful to their wives. He was never unfaithful to me, and had he been, I'm sure that I would have known. There would have been some break in the feeling of trust and security that I felt with him. He was a good husband who cherished me and loved me. I guess his friends called him square and I suppose he died wondering whether he had missed anything. I only wish I had told him what a wonderful gift our marriage was to me. But I didn't know that until he was gone."

CHAPTER 9

Compulsive Male Personalities

"He must subdue her, absorb her, rip her apart and consume her."

Norman Mailer, *The Naked and the Dead*

There are some men who are obsessed with the idea of manhood. They present to the world aggressive, exaggerated male behaviour. In fact these men are really insecure, frightened of the feelings that they sometimes have, and determined to hide them. Such men are sometimes referred to as "compulsive male personalities." There are many variations of this behaviour, but the three most commonly met by women are Wife-Beaters, Casanovas, and Machos.

WIFE-BEATERS
We live in a society in which no intimate subject seems to be taboo in conversation except violence.

Yet violence is no stranger to us. It is estimated that one out of every hundred wives in Western society is a battered wife; that in Toronto, a city of over two million people, there are fifty thousand women who accept being beaten, kicked, and knocked about as part of marriage; that in one metropolitan community, 37 per cent of the women asking for a divorce cited physical brutality as the cause of their marriage breakdown.

What kind of men beat their wives? Labourers, lawyers, doctors, company presidents, plumbers, truck drivers. Wife-beaters are found in every class, every economic group, and every profession.

Professor Talcott Parsons explains this phenomenon in terms of the "compulsive masculine personality" - a by-product, he says, of homes in which the father is absent, and of the mobility and subsequent isolation of the nuclear family. As families scatter over greater distances, children are deprived of a supportive network of relatives to look to for role models. Instead, they are dependent on two adults, their mother and their father.

Within our society, a boy's relationship with his father all too often tends to be, at the best, vague. Father goes off to work every day. When he comes home, he is tired or preoccupied and the child is discouraged from bothering him. At school, most of his teachers are women. If his parents separate or divorce, his contact with his father may become even less frequent. The boy depends on his mother and identifies with her, but he knows he must grow up to be a man. Parsons writes:

> The boy has a tendency to form a direct feminine identification, since his mother is the model most readily available and significant to him. But he is not destined to become an adult woman. Moreover, he soon discovers that in certain vital respects women are considered to be inferior to men, that it would hence be shameful for him to grow up as a woman. Hence when boys emerge into what Freudians call the "latency period," their behavior tends to be marked by a kind of "compulsive masculinity."... Aggression toward wo-

men, who "after all are to blame," is an essential concomitant.

When there is no one in his life who can present him with a picture of a comfortable masculine identity, the adolescent boy overreacts in his desire to shut off his mother's influence and indulges in exaggerated toughness to prove that he is a man. If his mother is manless, she may encourage that behaviour. Some men never outgrow this pattern. When they marry, frustration triggers the compulsive masculine response. Whenever such a man loses control over his wife – if she pays attention to another man, makes a comment about his earning power, or seems, in however small a way, to be challenging him; or if some factor outside the marriage seems to belittle him – he resorts to physical brutality as the ultimate proof of his superiority and dominance.

Such a man is often unreasonably possessive. Just as he wanted to own his mother, to have her complete attention, so must he possess his wife. If she is pregnant, he beats her out of jealousy of the unborn child. He will turn on her if she is unfaithful – whether the infidelity is real or imagined makes no difference.

Many cases of wife-beating are linked to alcohol. A number of women involved in these situations admit that they felt that they could reform the man and tame his violence, within the context of a good marriage.

Often the violent man is the product of a violent marriage. His father may have beaten his mother; either of his parents may have beaten him. Statistics now seem to indicate that when a husband beats his wife, it is not unusual for her to pass along the violence and take out her frustration and rage by beating their children.

Why do the women stay? Most of the time, they stay for love. The beating is but one aspect of the man and, initially, it doesn't happen that often. Fear enters the picture. A woman may be afraid to leave, believing that

that will only enrage her husband even more. She may be unwilling to press charges, partly because she loves him, partly because she is financially dependent upon him and he will not be able to support his family if he is in jail, and partly because she fears even greater violence to her or her children when the proceedings are through. She may have such a low opinion of herself that she feels that this is the way she deserves to be treated. If she grew up in a home where violence was an accepted pattern of behaviour, she may accept her lot because she believes that all men and women behave this way.

She gets little protection from a society in which the phrase "rule of thumb" originated as a reference to the size of a switch that a husband was entitled to use to beat his wife. There are numerous references in legal history to the right of the husband to, for example, "chastise his wife with a whip or rattan no bigger than my thumb, in order to enforce the salutory restraints of domestic discipline." Although that particular law no longer holds, there are still many jurisdictions where, if the husband did to a stranger what he did to his wife, he would be charged with assault; yet the police or court will dismiss the action when imposed on a wife, treating it as a domestic dispute best ignored. In general, the police prefer to stay out of domestic arguments and seldom encourage a wife to press charges.

In many communities, the beaten wife stays with her husband because she has no other place to go. And in many large cities where there are hostels for women in need, she still returns to her husband before a solution has been found, because the need for space is so great that even when she has found a temporary refuge, she can't stay long.

Some people who have never been exposed to violence make judgements about such a woman: she must be sick, or she must like it, or she must have deserved it. In many cases, these women do suffer from low self-esteem, or have been exposed all their lives to a pattern of violence. But what they need from society is understanding and help, not blame: certainly not isolated blame that continues to perpetuate the belief that such behaviour is natural and understandable in a man. The man who beats his wife and/or children is also disturbed.

Wife-beating is not the same as the whips and ropes that are part of some couples' sado-masochistic sex lives. Wife-beating is abuse that affects the behaviour of future generations and it sometimes leads to the ultimate violence: murder. In some cases, the husband goes too far, and the result is a dead wife. In others, the wife, pushed beyond her limits, suddenly finds the situation intolerable and, in her rage, she commits murder.

CASANOVAS

Casanovas, those restless lovers who are constantly moving on to new conquests, move on for the same reason that men climb mountains: because women are there. The urge is irresistible; responding to it is made easier by the fact that the Casanova is, himself, almost always irresistible.

The Casanovas of this world are charming, intelligent, attractive men. They may not be handsome, but they have sex appeal. Since women not only respond to, but sometimes also throw themselves at men like this, the men might be forgiven for thinking that it is not only their right but their duty to share themselves with as many women as possible. To give one woman a monopoly on so much talent would surely be unfair to the rest of the female sex. For Casanova, spreading his sex appeal around means that he is able to experience over and over again the fever pitch that is inherent in the beginning of a sexual liaison. One can hardly blame a man then for starting out on the path of Don Juan. What discipline it would take to turn down so many opportunities. What self-sacrifice to give up so much pleasure!

Casanovas enchant their conquests – initially. So much experience gives these men expertise. So much desire to make a conquest creates romantic excitement. To win his way, a Casanova will say and do almost anything. He will tell a woman that she is beautiful, that she is the only one who brings him peace, that she drives him mad with passion, that he cares for her, that he will look after her, that he needs her. If he is young and unscrupulous, he may even use the word "love." The older he gets, the more he tries to avoid that word; but then the older he gets, the more he discovers how easy it is to avoid using it.

It is easy because women have an infinite capacity to imagine love. If a man courts a woman, is constantly at her door, sends flowers and poetry, and phones in the night to tell her he wants her, the woman decides that love must be present, even if it isn't articulated. Of course, she may have heard about his past tendency to constantly move on to new territory. Casanova probably told her about it himself. These men make it a point to warn women, to tell them about their past conquests, their (charming) irresponsibility, their failure to establish a lasting relationship. In fact, if there is one clue to recognition of a Casanova, it is his passionately murmured warning, usually given when you are naked and just about to make love: "Don't fall in love with me. I will only hurt you." Then, if the end of a relationship brings a scene, the gentleman uses his honesty as a screen for his conscience. He warned her; she wouldn't listen.

No warnings register with the emotionally immature woman. She believes that she can change him; that she can be the Scheherazade who will hold him for a thousand nights and beyond. Casanova may have loved hundreds of women and left them: he will love her and stay.

But move on he does, leaving behind a woman on the brink of a crack-up. She blames herself. There was something wrong with her; she failed to enchant. She is too fat, too thin, too boring, too stimulating, too demanding, too cool: not enough of a woman. Casanova, however, moves on regardless of the territory. Many of the women he meets and makes love to possess the qualities required to be glorious, stimulating, lifetime mates. But Casanova moves on, anyway. Why? Because he is a rogue, whose emotional development has been arrested at an adolescent stage.

Initially, he moves on because he needs the constant change and the stimulation of first-stage excitement, because the intrigue of multiple relationships and the delight in being so much to so many feeds his perpetually hungry ego. As he grows older, he moves on for different reasons, reasons that he may not be prepared to face. Because he has failed to grow, because he has no experience beyond the conquest stage of the male-female relationship, he doesn't know how to build something more permanent. What's more, while once he was a great stud, now excess has destroyed some of his powers. Unless he has the challenge of a new conquest, the excitement of a new body, the unadulterated admiration of a stranger, he is often impotent.

As he grows older, he discovers fear. Long-term relationships demand commitment. Once, when he was a young man, he might have had the potential for that commitment. Now that he is older, jaded in spirit, cynical in thought, his energy spent, he doesn't know whether he can find the faith, trust, and emotional energy that is needed to build a long-term relationship. He fears he doesn't have the personal depth to be able to do it. He is afraid to put himself to the test.

If Casanova's emotional development is arrested, so is his view of women. His script was written when he was young, when he was the predator and all women easy prey. No matter how old he grows, or which women he meets, he casts them all in the same mould. It never occurs to him that there might be a woman who would use him in exactly the same way he uses women.

Yet it happened, even to the original Casanova. There is a story about a woman, a complete stranger, who let that man into her carriage, where he proceeded from a squeeze of the hand to lovemaking before the ride was over. Some weeks later, Casanova met the lady in a friend's home. When she ignored him, he asked her if she had forgotten him. She replied, "I remember you perfectly, but a frolic does not constitute an introduction."

All Casanovas might remember that story. In his memoirs, the original Casanova mentions 116 mistresses by name and claims to have "possessed" hundreds of others. Bedded, perhaps, but not possessed. Casanovas never really possess a woman, never really know her, and certainly never understand what love is about. A man may be able to insinuate himself into a woman's bed, but it takes something more than charm and sexual technique to get inside her head, her heart, and her soul.

MACHOS

Machismo is a Latin word that celebrates the cult of virility. In some countries, like Mexico, where *machismo* is a deeply ingrained cultural phenomenon, it creates serious political and economic problems. There, the rising birthrate contributes to urban overcrowding and unemployment and slows the diffusion of educational and medical services. Reduction of that population growth, however necessary it may be for the good of the country, is a difficult process in a society where a man measures his manhood by the number of children (especially sons) whom he has spawned.

Although the roots of *machismo* go back to the Spanish conquistadors, who made the submission of local women part of their conquest of new lands, *machismo* is as much a part of the North American way as it is of the Latin American way. Harold Ballard, the doughty owner of the Toronto Maple Leafs hockey team, could not in any way be confused with a Latin lover. But when he told CBC broadcaster Barbara Frum to be quiet because women belonged on their backs, he was expressing a common North American version of *machismo*. Unfortunately for North American women, this version lacks the Latin fire that at least brings to female submission some compensating erotic authority. A Latin lover would know that there are many positions in which a man can keep a woman sexually subjugated: to restrict her to her back is a particularly unimaginative brand of *machismo*.

In the world as it is presently structured, a man must have some *machismo* in his soul in order to perform the functions society demands of him. But, if he accepts without question the traditional version of *machismo*, he shuts off his growth as a human being. For in that stereotype's portrayal of masculinity, there is no room for tenderness, softness, feelings. The traditional macho view polarizes masculine and feminine qualities, praising the masculine as strong, scorning the feminine as weak. To admit that every human being contains both masculine and feminine traits is impossible for the macho male: such an admission would not only undermine his image of himself as a superior person, but would also suggest the possibility of something he fears – homosexuality. Until a man comes to terms with *machismo*, until he is sure of his masculinity, until he can find a way to make *machismo* and humanity compatible, he will have uneasy relationships with all women – his mother, sisters, lovers, wife. Friendship with a woman will be impossible.

Some men have been able to grow beyond that locker-room version of *machismo*. A retired colonel and war hero expressed surprise that anyone today would define macho simply as "tough." "Macho contains it all," he said. For him, that may be possible, because his manhood has been tried under the grimmest rite of passage. But that is not true of all men.

Whether the practitioner is a flashing-eyed Latin *gau-*

cho, a loud-mouthed North American millionaire, or an uptight banker, the macho believes that man, and all masculine qualities, are superior to the female, and to all feminine qualities. He sees those qualities as sharply distinct: men are tough, strong, uncompromising; women are fragile, weak, lacking in logic. Because the macho man holds women and all things associated with women in contempt, he can never admit to any feelings, sensations, or thoughts that might, according to his strict definition, be considered feminine. The macho man would not, for instance, ever admit to fear.

If that seems extreme or out of date, in this world where so much emphasis has been placed on eliminating stereotypes, consider for example the training offered in St. John's private schools for boys operating in Manitoba, Alberta, and Ontario. The schools have been described as places with stiff regimes (including swatting with a paddle on a bare bottom for transgressions) and physical activities that, according to the Toronto *Globe and Mail*, are "designed to push the boys to their physical and mental limits to make men of them."

The physical demands of a St. John's education are so great that in 1976 a sixteen-year-old Toronto boy collapsed during a snowshoe trek from lack of body heat. He was pronounced dead in a Selkirk hospital, but was later revived. The following January, another sixteen-year-old had his feet frozen on a snowshoeing expedition; he was told to walk back to camp alone. In June of 1978, twelve St. John's boys, aged twelve to fourteen, died in a canoeing tragedy on Lake Timiskaming. A coroner's inquest revealed that the boys had gone on that trip without training in paddling or in canoe-overturning manoeuvres.

In an interview with Jane O'Hara of *The Toronto Sun*, Ted Byfield, a co-founder of the schools, said, "In the last five years we've taken the emphasis off the physical toughness and laid it onto spiritual fortitude. We found that the kids were interpreting toughness as a macho arrogance."

As the details of the canoeing tragedy were released and a challenge was issued for the survivors to go back to conquer the lake where their friends had died, I found myself wondering about the school's mission to turn boys into men. How much of a man should we expect a fourteen-year-old boy to be? And is this what it is to be a man? To attempt to demonstrate strength without first acquiring skill, without practising caution? To watch your comrades die and then, to prove that you are really tough, to go back to the scene to repeat the trip? In a macho world, perhaps, but not in a humane one.

The classic macho male does not permit himself to be in touch with his inner self. He lives instead by terms set out in a myth. This version of macho is a game played by men for other men – the adult version of Cock-of-the-Walk. This man will not be pushed around, ever. He has never learned to duck a fight, sees no wisdom in discretion, is sensitive to the possibility that anyone – a cab driver, a waiter, a passerby – might be taking advantage of him.

He enjoys nights out with the boys, watches one football game after another on television, and congregates with other men at parties. Yet he cannot articulate affection for his male friends and would not think of telling a buddy that he loved him, even when the emotion is present. Although the Latin macho can embrace his male friends, this is impossible for a North American man because of his fear of homosexuality. He restricts his touching of other men to vigorous back-thumping and works hard to develop a bone-breaking handshake.

The macho man is intolerant of and often aggressively hostile toward homosexuals. Even when they are not bothering him, he seems threatened by their presence. They remind him perhaps of qualities he has buried in his subconscious, qualities he has not yet come to terms with.

Without ever having seen it, the macho man knows that he hates the ballet. Because the strength and skill of the male ballet dancer comes packaged with beautiful music, sensitivity, and romantic costumes, the macho male rejects the idea that a male ballet dancer could be masculine. The father of one of the brightest young stars in Canadian ballet never could reconcile himself to his son's career. Even when the boy had achieved success, the father was so distressed by the homosexual connotation of ballet that he refused to watch his offspring perform, despite the fact that his son is clearly heterosexual in his interests.

The macho man looks after his woman to such an extent that she is discouraged from working for money, even if her wages are needed, for fear that someone will question his ability to provide. If his wife does work, it is understood that her work is not as important as his. If a child is sick, she takes the day off. If the child has a problem at school, it is she, not he, who finds the time to visit the principal. If she is offered a promotion that involves relocating the family, there is no question of her accepting it; she turns it down. He loves her when he feels like it, leaves her when he feels like it, and talks about her to others (usually deprecatingly) if he chooses to do so. He admits to no tenderness, no sentiment, no need for anyone else, and certainly never to the need to be held and comforted in the middle of the night.

In his sex life, the macho male initiates and orchestrates. He is confident that he is a good lover, would not consider accepting instruction, is against marriage counselling. He is free to make love to as many women as he likes – that is, after all, a man's nature. In extreme cases, he has been known to take a casual sexual encounter home and demand that his wife make breakfast for her. His wife, however, is permitted no infidelity. Let her stray once, no matter what the circumstances, and he either uses her indiscretion as an excuse for a lifetime of promiscuous and cruel behaviour, or he throws her out loudly, for all the world to hear.

One very wealthy businessman chose to do the latter. He and his wife had been married for twenty-five years. During that time he had travelled extensively and his spouse had been a model wife, running a magnificent home, playing a part in the community, entertaining graciously, raising two children. She was left alone for long periods of time, so no one was surprised to hear that she had fallen in love with someone and embarked on an affair. When her husband found out, he threw her out.

Shortly thereafter, he and I had dinner, and I spent most of the evening trying to persuade him that he should consider a reconciliation. His wife's affair had ended. She was repentant and anxious to get her marriage back together.

He looked at me as if I had grown another head. "Don't you realize," he said, "that my wife was unfaithful to me?"

I argued back. "But David, you have spent at least six months of every year away from your family, travelling on business. Are you telling me that you were never unfaithful to Julie?"

"Of course," he replied, "I slept with other women. But I never slept with another woman twice." That, I thought, was a curious, macho version of fidelity.

The macho man sees every woman as a possible sexual conquest. To him, making a pass is an automatic gesture. He cannot accept a woman as a friend, a partner, or an equal. Let him meet a woman who has accomplished something and he is at once competitive, determined to reduce her to an inferior state.

Caroline: "I met Bruno through mutual friends. I was attracted to him right away. He was obviously very successful and he seemed sure of himself, very strong. I responded to that.

"We went to dinner several times that first week, but despite the fact that we were sexually attracted, we didn't go to bed. When he went away on business, we were separated for three weeks. That separation accelerated our desire. He phoned me every day, sent me long and romantic letters. When we met again, we became lovers and the lovemaking was exquisite. I fell in love with him.

"He was involved in a project in which there was a need for my professional skill. I volunteered to help, partly because I loved him and wanted to help him, to be part of his life, and partly because working together would give me an excuse to travel with him. I couldn't face another separation. I wanted him to be proud of me as well as to love me, so I worked very hard, using all my contacts, putting everything I had into the job. And I did a good job. We landed several big contracts through people I introduced him to.

"The more successful I was, the worse he treated me. He began to criticize my clothes, my hair, my jewelry, my friends. He belittled my work, not only in private, but in front of people. He wouldn't admit that I had made a contribution to his business. He couldn't admit that anything I had done had paid off. He kept finding flaws.

"His lovemaking became cruder, rougher. It was as though he was trying to break me in some way. He would go for hours without speaking to me, would deliberately flirt with another woman in a restaurant, and would get into bed without kissing me. I became more and more nervous as I tried to humour him, or to jolly him into a good mood. I was constantly on the verge of tears, wondering what I'd done wrong. I couldn't stand it any longer. I just checked out of the hotel and flew home, without even saying goodbye.

"He was furious, of course. He phoned me and yelled that I had abandoned him. He criticized my professionalism as well as my manners."

Identifying certain macho men is easy. There are the body-magnificent jocks and the successful rock stars who take sexual advantage of the groupies who adore them; the leather-jacketed bikers who talk scornfully of their old ladies; even the Archie-Bunker men of the business world, with their narrow view of female talent, are quickly spotted. But in the corporate world, there is a much more sophisticated version of the macho male who is harder to identify. This man may not have a macho physique. Instead of being barrel-chested and tight-bellied, he may have sloping shoulders and slack stomach muscles. His macho game is not sport, but power.

He turns his back on heart, something that he identifies as feminine, to concentrate on head, which he usually regards as masculine. His brand of macho means staying in control, detached from emotions. This business stance soon spreads into other parts of his life, making intimate relationships with family or friends impossible. He is not likely to indulge in the same activities as his more openly macho cousin. He will be found more often at an elegant dinner table than in a recreation room watching football on television. He drinks wine instead of beer and can eat an artichoke with grace. But in every phase of his life, he must dominate, control, lay down the rules, call the shots. In that, he is as macho as his Mexican peasant counterpart.

I have known many men who live their lives according to macho rules. Most of them are frauds.

They put so much energy into brawling, making a noisy show of arch-masculinity, and seeking to dominate, that they have no energy left for friendship, love, fatherhood, personal growth. They are so busy counting scores with women that they fail to consider whether they ever had any genuine successes. The macho myth is concerned only with making women, not with making them satisfied. Numbers are so important to macho males that they don't care whether they are accurate-

making other men think that they have scored is as important as actually scoring.

One such man was very candid with me about that. A young and attractive television host, he phoned me after my separation to ask me out. After several phone calls, I said to him, "I'd like to go to the theatre with you as long as you realize that I am emotionally involved with someone else. I'd want it to be clear from the start that there will be no sex, because I don't want any late-night hassles."

"That's okay," he said. "If you go out with me everyone will think we are having an affair, and that's good enough." I wish I could tell you that he was indulging himself in some wry humour, but he wasn't - he was deadly serious.

As for tears, some of the most macho strutters I have known have been the most maudlin of weepers. They may never shed a tear over a poem or a tender moment, but they cry endless tears of self-pity. Not in the locker room with their peers, of course, but late at night in an emptying bar you can find Sir Macho crying on the shoulder of a concerned lady friend. She is too polite to admit to her boredom as he cries over lost powers, lost opportunities, lost loves, lost marriages, lost friendships, and lost chances to grow.

And why shouldn't he grow? Or cry? He has allowed himself to be the victim of the worst myth of all: the belief that in order to be a real man, he must deny all feeling.

How different it would be if such men would realize that life's most challenging task is to become a fully developed human being. It takes courage to risk growth and to encounter feelings; maturity to accept responsibility for those feelings and the actions that they provoke. The man who can do this, the man who can admit to his humanity, is the man a woman thinks of as strong.

A WOMAN'S MACHO MAN

A woman's ideal macho man is courageous enough to sometimes admit to fear; potent enough to admit that he is sometimes helpless, that he cannot hold back age, illness, death, or the perversities of fate; tough enough to be tender sometimes; stable enough to permit a woman to lean; and honest enough to sometimes lean himself. This is a man whose virility is so unquestioned that he is not afraid to read poetry, respond to a symphony, admire the beauty in the soaring of a bird. He may even decide that living things are too beautiful to hunt for sport; this decision will come not from what a conventional macho male would consider sissy-squeamishness-but from conviction rooted in principles.

The macho man a woman loves to love is the man who loves her and stays-not necessarily forever, but long enough to take coupling out of the animal kingdom and put it back into the realm of human communication. And if this macho man talks about lovemaking he talks to her, in the quiet of their bed, not to the boys in the locker room, because he is manly enough to know that privacy lends lustre to lovemaking. Cheap talk makes it cheap.

A woman's macho male is not afraid to tackle what can be a lifelong task: building one adult relationship with one woman. He does not think fidelity a feminine preoccupation. He knows that with three hundred women, he can use the same gambit over and over again. But to satisfy one woman three hundred times-that requires real *machismo*.

CHAPTER 10

Variations in the Male Orgasm

"The penis is the only limb or 'member' which defies the control of the will, which, that is, actually has a will of its own rising and falling of its own accord and not, like the arms or the lips, at the dictate of the owner's will."

Saint Augustine

There have been countless books and articles written about female sexuality. The experts have explained that women need foreplay if they are to achieve orgasm; that the physical and the emotional are closely related in a woman; that certain conditions can adversely affect female response; that a woman can go through the act of intercourse without achieving orgasm and, in some circumstances, still be comfortable and happy, while in others she will feel dissatisfied and frustrated; that she may be multi-orgasmic, experiencing climax after climax, and that each climax may vary in intensity.

Very little, however, is written about the wide range of variations possible in the male sexual response. As a result, many women assume that a male orgasm is like Gertrude Stein's rose - the same for every man, every time, with every partner. These women believe that men can, and always do, separate the emotional from the physical. They assume that the male orgasm is unvarying in its intensity and that when a man has sex, orgasm – and pleasure – are automatic. Along with many men, these women believe orgasm and ejaculation to be the same thing. Yet they are not only different and separate, but it is also not uncommon for a man to have one without experiencing the other.

THE DIFFERENCE BETWEEN ORGASM AND EJACULATION

Doctors Avinoam and Beryl Chernick are a husband-and-wife team of sex therapists with a private practice in London, Ontario. Avinoam Chernick says, "There is no such thing as a standard male orgasm. There may be a fantastic orgasm and fantastic ejaculation; there may be a good orgasm with a dribbly ejaculation or it may be the other way around. If a man hasn't ejaculated for a very long time he may not have a very intense orgasm with a great deal of ejaculate. Ejaculation and orgasm are neurologically different functions. Each is felt in a different place and there is a different quality to each sensation.

"Women have talked for several years about their ability to have multiple orgasms. But a guy with absolute control also has the capability, if he's properly trained, to be multi-orgasmic, and then finish with an ejaculation. That's possible when a man learns to control the split orgasm-ejaculation function."

It is also possible for a man to experience both ejaculation and orgasm and still not feel satisfied. "I hear about that kind of lack of satisfaction in the context of an ineffective relationship," Chernick says. "If a woman makes it clear to a man that he is taking too long, that she is not interested, that she has other things to do, the man may experience orgasm and ejaculation without satisfaction. With men as well as women, the body, the brain, and the emotions are tied together. It's almost impossible to tell where one begins and another leaves off."

Chernick's comments make it clear that the male has as wide a range of sexual function and dysfunction as the female and that a man's sexual response is not at all fixed. It will vary according to age and physical change, as well as emotional and psychological factors.

No two men are alike. According to Chernick, their capacity to involve themselves in the act of lovemaking varies from "the man who is completely involved with his partner and attached to her from the early stage of sex play throughout the various excitement, plateau, orgasm, and resolution phases of sex, to the guy who is only there physically. Mentally he is making love to his previous wife, or to the only woman who has ever turned him on, or sometimes to the boy next door."

What about the myth that says that if you put a bag over a woman's head, a man can still make love to her? Chernick says, "That probably applies to some men, but very few. When we start scraping away all the layers of lard off that, you'll find the same range of sensitivity in men that you find in women. Some men are totally insensitive to all but the physical. But then there are some women who can sleep with any guy, too."

THE AGE FACTOR

The physical characteristics of the male sexual pattern vary according to a man's age. Chernick explains that a male infant can have an erection in response to tactile stimulation of the abdomen and thighs. "A nine-year-old can have an erection and orgasm without any pressure to ejaculate. Because of that he can enjoy prolonged sex play – peeking, touching, necking – without any genital stimulation, and still experience pleasure. But when his system has matured, say at age fifteen, the physical pressure to ejaculate becomes intense. In a sense, the need to ejaculate gets in the way of lovemaking. When ejaculation becomes the focus, the sensual side goes undeveloped. At fifteen, a boy has fast recovery, so he can get an erection and ejaculate four or five times in a short period of time. But where the nine-year-old can go on playing with himself all day, having a lovely time, even the fifteen-year-old eventually has to rest, because ejaculation requires more effort, more protein than an orgasm."

Some men never get past the fifteen-year-old stage of sexual development. They are self-taught rapid ejaculators, always in such a hurry to get to the end that they miss the pleasure along the way. Beryl Chernick says that these men are so focussed on ejaculation that they are completely out of touch with a whole gradation of feelings – genital feelings, sensual feelings and, usually, other kinds of feelings as well. Sometimes this is the result of peer pressure: a how-many-times-can-you-do-it competition akin to how many hot dogs you can eat at one sitting. More often it is the product of fear of discovery. Just as an animal in the wild ejaculates quickly because he wants to reduce the length of time he is vulnerable to predators, so a teenager will masturbate to a fast ejaculation for fear that his mother might come into his room. Later, he's in a hurry because a police officer might check the back of his car or because he is worried that his date's father – or husband – will come home.

When he marries, he continues to make love in this pattern, depending on what the Chernicks call "double or triple headers" to satisfy his mate. That can work – until the machinery starts to slow down. When he's thirty or forty, with increasing business and financial pressures, a deteriorating physical condition, and a higher intake of alcohol, his ability to recover slows down. After achieving the fast ejaculation that is his pattern, he may find that it takes too long to get another erection: his wife has gone to sleep, unsatisfied.

Age is often the cure for that. Chernick explains, "As a man gets older, two changes occur. His muscle tone decreases and his congestion goes down. It takes him longer to get an erection. There is less pressure for him to ejaculate, so he has more time for love play. If he can satisfactorily make use of this time, then the relationship can really grow sexually at this stage of life, just because of the physiological changes going on."

Those physiological changes may mean that the man doesn't get an erection as quickly. The erection may not be as firm, or it may become totally firm only just before orgasm. His orgasm may not be as intense and he may not ejaculate as much fluid. But the decrease in his need to ejaculate will permit him to take more time with his lovemaking, and he will experience an increase in satisfaction from sex play. His orgastic pattern changes. Instead of having deep orgasm followed by ejaculatory contractions, he may have small ejaculatory contractions and deep orgasm, or one without the other: sometimes, neither. But the comforting thing is that, because of the changes in his body, he may not need to ejaculate or experience orgasm to know either pleasure or satisfaction.

With both men and women, the resolution phase occurs much more quickly as they get older. After orgasm, they can then experience immediate satisfaction and comfort. Throughout all these stages, there is a wide spectrum of sexual performance. At one end of the scale, there is the ideal stud who can easily achieve, maintain, and control his erection. At the other, there is the man who has no competence with his penis at all.

SOME SEXUAL DYSFUNCTIONS

The most obvious sexual dysfunction is the inability to obtain or maintain an erection. This may be a general inability or it may be an inability with a specific woman. Sometimes a man can obtain an erection and have an ejaculation, but not in conjunction with a vagina. He may be able to ejaculate only against a door, or face-down on a sheet.

Very often, this is the result of fear. That fear may be a

primitive concern for what will happen to his poor penis once it is inside the vagina - does it have teeth? Or it may be a fear of getting hurt or a fear of hurting. There may be a profound concern for the possibility of pregnancy. Above all, there may be a fear that the man will be inadequate as a lover, that he will fail to satisfy his partner. This will be heightened if his view of a man is someone who always comes to a woman with an erect penis. Some men cannot recognize the flaccid penis as a legitimate organ and they are ashamed if they need the assistance of their partners to achieve an erection.

Another form of sexual dysfunction involves the timing of a man's ejaculation. If he has not learned to control the timing of that, then he may come too soon, before either he or his partner is ready. Lasting longer is a learned response, a matter of discipline. A man knows when he is approaching the point of inevitability. With training, he can make a decision to stop everything. He can decrease his reactions, he can decide to have non-ejaculatory contractions, or he can decide to ejaculate.

Some men are not able to ejaculate at all and this can be as difficult for a man as an ejaculation that is uncontrolled. Sometimes this is a function of age, occurring when a man is fifty, sixty, or seventy. In this case it is not so worrisome, because very often the man will find that he doesn't need an ejaculation in order to experience pleasure.

The inability to ejaculate may also be caused by medical factors; it occurs sometimes immediately after a prostectomy. But there may be deep-rooted, very human causes. The dysfunction may be the result of being physically or emotionally beaten. Sometimes, it happens to men who make a fetish of love play. Each time this man has intercourse it takes longer and requires more and more stimulation to achieve the same sexual response. Occasionally, the cause is a poor physical match; if the penis is small and the vagina large, there may not be enough stimulation (unless the woman provides it manually) to bring about ejaculation.

MALE FANTASIES
Men have sexual fantasies that are as varied as the human imagination. They may revolve around extreme discipline; such a man will want his partner to order him around, to humiliate him, to tie him up - or he may want to discipline his partner in that way. Some men like to be babied, to nurse for hours, to be petted. Other fantasies revolve around the choice of partner in endless variation - animals, different men, different women, men and women together, a daughter and a grandmother, a mother and a daughter. Some fantasies are about stimulation - oral stimulation, anal stimulation, or wild and exotic positions. No matter how bizarre or far-fetched the method of sexual intercourse, some man, somewhere, has already dreamed about it.

CHAPTER 11

What Makes a Good Lover?

"Love is perhaps but gratitude for pleasure."

Honoré de Balzac

Most men are poor lovers.

Sometimes this is because they confuse lovemaking with what they call "fucking."

A few years ago, I was having dinner with two men, one a California composer, the other a Canadian television executive.

The TV chief was telling a long tale of corporate woe about someone who had double-crossed him in a meeting. He ended the conversation with a description of the curse he wanted to put on the enemy.

"Fuck him," he said.

The Californian leaned across the table and replied, "But Gordon, if you don't like the man and you're wishing him ill, surely it would be more appropriate if you said, 'Almost fuck him.' No one should wish anything as marvellous as a fuck on an enemy."

There you have an example of the wide variation in

meanings ascribed to that famous four-letter word. To the Californian, the word "fuck" is not derogatory; used the way he would use it, between two lovers under private circumstances, that old Anglo-Saxon word is still rich in nuance, meaning, and emotion.

But to most men, "fuck" is a swear word and when a man swears at a woman, either verbally or with his penis, he gives her no pleasure.

PENIS-ORIENTED MEN

There are some men, of course, who make a sharp distinction between lovemaking and intercourse. Convinced that sex is something dirty and sinful, they deliberately separate the two, choosing a different woman for each. These are the men with the madonna-whore approach to women. Wives are for loving – without imagination and as quickly as possible. Whores, paid or unpaid, are for sexual relief.

This attitude is encouraged by the tendency of some men to see their penises as something quite apart from the rest of themselves. They often carry this separation to the extreme of giving their sexual organ a name of its own. Lady Chatterley's lover called his John Thomas. The modern gamekeeper may refer to it as Dick, Sampson, or That Rascal. He may take his cue from Henry Miller and think of his penis as It; he may refer to it as his pecker; or he may christen it with the name of a Crusader hero. But once the penis has its own name, its owner has symbolically separated himself from his responsibility for his sexual drive. His penis is something that embarrassed him regularly when he was an adolescent, and sometimes still does; it is often out of control, does not think, has no judgement and leads its reluctant owner down paths that are beyond his responsibility.

In order to become a good lover, a man must grow beyond this attitude. He must not only assume responsibility for his sexuality, he must integrate it with his emotions, his intellect, and his soul. To do that, he will have to overcome many myths, some of them nurtured by literature, some of them encouraged by the silence of women, others created for men by men in locker rooms. Out of these myths there comes a group of men who mistakenly believe that the ability to make love is determined by the penis.

This penis-oriented man is almost always worried about his sexual equipment - its size, its hardness, its staying power, its ability to perform on command, its eagerness to repeat the performance. These qualities may have merit in the locker room: they are the way one man measures another as a sexual competitor. But they mean nothing in the bedroom. They are not the way a woman measures a man as a lover. And until a man cares more about what pleases a woman than he does about what will impress other men, he might be able to have sex, but he will know nothing about making love.

PERFORMANCE-ORIENTED MEN

The performance-oriented man believes that all physical contact should lead to sex. As a result, he is unable to touch simply for the sake of touching. He denies himself the pleasure of non-sexual stroking - something all human beings need - and shortchanges his mate of it as well. He may well be unreasonably possessive. Because he is concerned that his penis might not be normal, he lives in fear that someday his mate might be able to make a comparison that would not be to his advantage. This may explain why male frontal nudity is almost taboo, although exposure of the female genitals is commonplace, in film as well as in art.

He is quick to suspect infidelity. Let the woman be unusually responsive, or let her initiate something new, and his puritan classification system goes to work. If she is exuberant in her enjoyment of sex, if she has some knowledge not learned through him, she must have been unfaithful. His sexual exploration is further hampered by his belief that a real man always leads the woman. Let her show a desire to initiate lovemaking, take a position on top, or be aggressive in other ways, and he is turned off. He fears that in trying to take away what he sees as his rightful function, the woman is trying to castrate him.

Many men are closet romantics, some are much more romantic than women are. It is, after all, men who buy black nightgowns on Christmas Eve and women who take them back on Boxing Day. Yet the penis-oriented man denies this part of himself. The myth says that the penis does not discriminate, that it should always be in the mood, willing. When a man accepts that as truth, he denies himself the right to be sensitive to surroundings and circumstances – let alone to be weary or in need of a loving cuddle rather than intercourse.

This man is the most vulnerable of all men. His penis only has credibility when it is aroused; flaccid, it has no existence. Let that penis just once be tired, and suddenly the gap between the man and his organ closes. His entire identity is threatened.

Let him once be impotent and his panic can be so severe that a justifiable response to fatigue, alcohol, the wrong atmosphere, or the wrong woman is worried into a continuing condition requiring professional help. When a man is experiencing sexual difficulties, it becomes clear that his ignorance of the female body is matched only by his ignorance of the working of his own. He is disconcerted to discover that he can have an erection without wanting to have sex; that he can ejaculate without experiencing pleasure, and does not know that this is not abnormal.

THE PENIS MYTH
The myth of the all-important penis has hampered the development of men as lovers in many ways. First, this

theory leads a man to believe that the presence of an erect penis is all that is required to satisfy a woman. If that conviction is strong enough, he never bothers to learn anything about female anatomy. He assumes that he was born with whatever knowledge he needs to be a lover and that that knowledge is stored between his legs. This is the man who believes that getting it up and putting it in is enough to please a woman.

Some women have encouraged this myth. Indeed, what is so surprising about the spate of books dealing with female sexuality is not that so many men are such unsatisfactory lovers, but that so many women have been quiet about it for so long. For a variety of reasons - including inhibitions, self-blame, an inability to articulate feelings, and a sexual response based on getting it over with as soon as possible - women have "faked it." And men have believed them. In that faking, as in all dishonesty, women hurt not only men but also themselves. In this case, the ripples of their dishonesty have touched their sisters.

Now we have gone to the other extreme. Where once women would say nothing, now we say too much in far too strident tones. Some New Women make it clear that they will do the choosing and that they will set the standard, demanding orgasm after orgasm, clocking performance. In their response to this all men are very nearly alike. They are turned off - sometimes turned off one woman to another, sometimes turned off sex to impotence, and sometimes from heterosexuality to homosexuality.

Literature has played its part in exaggerating the importance of the penis in lovemaking. Male writers from Henry Miller to Norman Mailer and Harold Robbins endow their heros with enormous, angry sex organs whose presence alone is enough to bring the always passive woman to ecstasy. In *Sexus*, Miller writes, "I poked it around inside her like a demon, up, sideways, down, in." That idea might excite Henry Miller but I know of no woman who has ever found pleasure in the presence of a penis poking around.

Emphasizing the athletic aspect of the penis has encouraged men to be dazzled by a sexual track record. A few years ago, a story circulated to the effect that author Georges Simenon claimed to have made love to ten thousand women. Men were so astonished at this, so envious, and so full of admiration that penis-oriented managing editors gave the item front-page space in newspapers around the world.

My first thought was that we had heard only half the story. What about the women? Shouldn't they be allowed to comment? Perhaps Simenon was such a terrible lover that no woman would let him near her twice. Copulation with ten thousand women certainly indicates that a man has a successful approach, that he is attractive and energetic. It establishes quantity, but it says nothing about quality. I would be much more impressed if one woman were to step forward and say, "Georges Simenon satisfied me ten thousand times." That would prove he was a good lover.

One wonders why men are so concerned with meeting male standards when it is women who are their partners. It is not men who should be giving out certificates of sexual prowess to themselves or to other men. That is an honour only a woman can bestow. And women are not penis-oriented. I know of no woman who has ever found fault with a man as a lover because of the shape, size, or endurance of his penis. Indeed, it is quite possible for her to be satisfied without the attentions of one. Nor is she disconcerted when presented with a lifeless organ – making it grow through her efforts can bring her both sensual pleasure and a heady sense of power.

THE 13 FEATURES OF A GOOD LOVER
Some men are excellent lovers.

There is no formula for that: the chemistry, needs, desires, and imaginations of each individual couple determine the basis of excellence in lovemaking. Taste also enters: what one woman considers exciting - being tied to a bed with satin ribbons and spanked - another might find repugnant, or too silly to be sexy.

Yet, even accounting for variations in taste, there is agreement about certain fundamentals of a good lover.

1. The good lover is reasonably happy with himself. Bed for him is a place for pleasure, not a proving ground or a battlefield.

2. He is physically clean and takes good care of his health and his body. He is discreet and discriminating.

3. The good lover is not afraid to feel; he is willing to risk emotional exposure; he welcomes intimacy.

4. He is considerate of the circumstances of a woman's life and protective of her. If she is single with children and does not want to make love under their roof, he respects that. If she is his wife and is exhausted from housework, he helps remove some of that pressure so that she has more energy for sex.

5. He recognizes a woman's vulnerability. He does not protest that he does not want to get involved and then proceed to bind her to him with lovemaking that implies otherwise.

6. The good lover does not wait until he gets into bed to make love. He courts a woman first - by remembering her between meetings with phone calls, letters; by engaging in preliminaries like non-sexual touching and flirtation. He does not leap on a woman, unless it is clear that there has been so much longing in their separation that neither can wait.

7. He does not consider sex to be an area in which the male must dominate. He is willing to learn from his

partner, explore with her, is prepared to alternate between the submissive and the aggressive, and does not feel threatened if she takes the initiative.

8. He is willing to assume some of the responsibility for birth control and is committed to helping his partner with the decision and the course of action should a pregnancy occur.

9. The good lover talks to his mate. He speaks about his feelings, about his pleasure in his woman, before he makes love, as well as during and afterwards. He does not, however, talk about what is between them to others, nor does he tell her about other women – past, present, or possible.

10. He is sensual. He likes to touch and taste, to linger over lovemaking. He does not consider foreplay to be a prescribed routine to follow the way he might paint by number; he thinks of loveplay as a delicious part of the whole act, a pleasure in itself.

11. He understands female anatomy and knows how to help a woman achieve orgasm. Her pleasure intensifies his excitement.

12. The good lover does not leap out of bed after his own orgasm. He stays with a woman, holding her, talking with her, sharing a glass of wine, a cigarette, or a bath.

13. Nor does he go abruptly out of her life. If he is a husband, he kisses his wife goodbye the next morning in a way that recalls the lovemaking of the night before. If he is a lover, he telephones.

No matter what events might separate them, a man and a woman who have shared excellent lovemaking will always respond to each other when one is in need, for they are bound together by the strongest of bonds: the memory of pleasure.

CHAPTER 12

The Loving Men

"having loved, thou lovest to the end."

Elizabeth Barrett Browning

All men are not alike. That's what makes them - and life - so interesting.

I have loved and been loved by several men. Most of that love came within the framework of cherished, valued, continuing friendships. Twice, it was an all-encompassing emotion that involved all of my senses and altered my perspective on myself, my world, and life.

I have not written about those loving men, except in general terms, because such relationships deserve privacy. If I have dwelled in this book on men who have problems relating to women, it is not to suggest that they represent all men. There are many well adjusted, responsible, giving men out there. It is, after all, the performance of the loving men that gives women something to measure the difficult ones by.

Nor should this book be interpreted as evidence that I don't like men. I do; so much so that I would like to help improve what goes on between men and women. I feel sorry for men. Women are skilled at talking about themselves, at analyzing their needs and their anxieties and articulating their wants. They may not have achieved much progress in solving their problems, but at least they have brought the problems out in the open. Men, on the other hand, are not encouraged to be introspective about their longings. As a rule, they don't talk about such things. Because they don't talk about their feelings, some women leap to the conclusion that men don't have feelings.

The women's movement has focussed attention on the stereotyping of women and on how inhibiting that has been for them. It has verbalized the problems women face in trying to develop individual identities. But little attention has been paid to the obvious corollary that men, too, have been stereotyped, trapped, and moulded into something less than human. That they participated in the creation of the myths that entrap them only makes it harder for men to break out.

What is needed is understanding: understanding of the intense pressure and unremitting demands that society has placed on men; understanding of the impossible standards men have demanded of themselves; understanding that the wants, needs, and expectations of men and women have much more in common than in contrast.

What is needed is honesty. Not the "let-it-all-hang-out, I'm-going-to-say-this-even-if-it-hurts-you" kind of honesty; but loving, sharing truth that contributes to growth. Who can have sympathy for a woman who says at the end of a marriage, "You never satisfied me"? Surely there was a place, somewhere in the early stages of that loving, when she could have demonstrated to her mate how he might satisfy her. Surely there is a way that men can be encouraged to say what they feel, and surely society will give them permission to admit that they sometimes need and want a romantic atmosphere with sex.

THE DEADLY MYTHS

It is time to say goodbye to some of the myths that have kept men out of touch, not only with women, but with themselves. What myths?

The myth that women have a monopoly on feeling; that men do not feel tenderness, cannot love their children; that a man should not admit to his feelings, that he must accept all that comes with stoic, controlled behaviour.

The myth that a man separates the physical from the emotional; that all sex leads a man to pleasure; that a real man is always in the mood to make love.

The myth that sex is male territory; that a man should initiate it, determine the content, and assume responsibility for his partner's orgasm, as well as his own.

The myth that there is such a thing as instant intimacy, that either sex can find warmth and safety without commitment.

The myth that men are rovers and women are faithful. Promiscuity doesn't have any gender; neither does the capacity to commit oneself to a life-long relationship.

The belief that a man always wants to chase a woman. As George Sand wrote, "Obstacles usually stimulate passion, but sometimes they kill it." There are moments when a woman should be the aggressor.

The myth of superiority. The sexes are not in competition, they are not designed to be dominant and inferior; they are designed to be complementary. Each of us has masculine and feminine qualities. We should not deny those attributes.

The belief, on the part of many women, that men should somehow be able to divine women's needs and should automatically know what pleases them and would make them happy.

The myth of belonging: that all it takes to make us happy is someone's love; that we can find our identity in the eyes of a beloved; that love means ownership and total identification: the giving up of self.

Above all, we must guard against judging the men and women we meet by past experiences, against concluding that all men are alike or that all women are the same. Somehow, we must learn to analyze ourselves so that we stop seeking out the same kind of failure-prone relationship, and then blaming that failure on the opposite sex.

The only things more marvellous than our own individuality are the endless possibilities offered in relationships. Each man and each woman, when they join together, become a unique couple whose love is like no other couple's love; they form a relationship in which they create their own dimension.

Bibliography

Simone de Beauvoir, *The Second Sex* (New York: Alfred A. Knopf, Inc., 1953).

Eugene C. Bianchi and Rosemary Radford Ruether, *From Machismo to Mutuality* (New York: Paulist Press, 1976).

Henry Biller, *Paternal Deprivation* (Lexington, Mass.: D.C. Heath, 1974).

Marie Borland, ed., *Violence in the Family* (Atlantic Highlands, N.J.: Humanities Press, 1976).

Beryl Chernick and Avinoam Chernick, *In Touch* (Toronto: Macmillan of Canada, 1977).

Marc Feigen Fasteau, *The Male Machine* (New York: McGraw-Hill Book Company, 1974).

Margaret Hennig and Anne Jardim, *The Managerial Woman* (New York: Doubleday Publishing Company, 1977).

Seymour B. Liebman, *Exploring the Latin American Mind* (Chicago: Nelson-Hall Inc., 1976).

Michael Macoby, *The Gamesman* (New York: Bantam Books, 1978).

William H. Masters et al., *The Pleasure Bond* (New York: Bantam Books, 1976).

Sigmund Stephen Miller, *The Good Life, Sexually Speaking* (Englewood Cliffs, N.J.: Prentice-Hall, Inc., 1972).

Ashley Montagu, *The Natural Superiority of Women* (New York: Macmillan Publishing Company, 1968).

Avodah K. Offet, *The Sexual Self* (Philadelphia: J.B. Lippincott Co., 1977).

Talcott Parsons, *Essays in Sociological Theory* (New York: Collier-Macmillan, 1954).

Anthony Pietropinto and Jacqueline Simmenauer, *Beyond the Male Myth* (New York: Times Books, 1977).

Suzanne K. Steinmetz and Murray A. Straus, *Violence in the Family* (New York: Harper and Row, 1974).

Linda Wolfe, *Playing Around* (New York: William Morrow and Co., Inc., 1975).

Acknowledgements

My thanks to the women who talked so openly to me about their relationships with men. As promised, their identities have been disguised beyond all recognition; to Doctors Avinoam and Beryl Chernick, who not only provided me with information about male sexuality but also have done so much to help couples all over North America to understand each other; to Deborah Anne Sutton, who assisted with some of the research and the typing of the manuscript; to Dr. Lillian Messinger of the Clarke Institute of Psychiatry, who shared her valuable research into the problems of separated and divorced fathers; to Denise Bukowski, who cosseted not only the manuscript, but its author; and to the men in my life who have helped me to understand that all men are definitely not alike.